The Syntax of Words

The Syntax of Words

Elisabeth O. Selkirk

The MIT Press
Cambridge, Massachusetts
London, England

Second MIT Press paperback edition, April 1983

© 1982 by The Massachusetts Institute of Technology

This book was set in VIP Times Roman by Village Typographers, Inc., and printed and bound by Halliday Lithograph in the United States of America.

Library of Congress Cataloging in Publication Data

Selkirk, Elisabeth O., 1945–
  The syntax of words.

  (Linguistic inquiry monographs ; 7)
  Bibliography: p.
  Includes index.
  1. Grammar, Comparative and general—Morphology. 2. Grammar, Comparative and general—Syntax. 3. Generative grammar. 4. English language—Word formation. I. Title. II. Series.
P241.S44 1983   415   82–17122
ISBN 0–262–19210–1
ISBN 0–262–69079–9 (pbk.)

Contents

Contents

Series Foreword

We are pleased to present this monograph as the seventh in the series *Linguistic Inquiry Monographs*. These monographs will present new and original research beyond the scope of the article, and we hope they will benefit our field by bringing to it perspectives that will stimulate further research and insight.

Originally published in limited edition, the *Linguistic Inquiry Monograph* series is now available on a much wider scale. This change is due to the great interest engendered by the series and the needs of a growing readership. The editors wish to thank the readers for their support and welcome suggestions about future directions the series might take.

Samuel Jay Keyser
for the Editorial Board

Preface

It may be useful to trace the history of this monograph in the interest of bibliographical clarity. I drafted a first version in 1977, intending to include it as a chapter in my forthcoming book *Phonology and Syntax: The Relation between Sound and Structure*. Its purpose was to lay out a backdrop of assumptions concerning word structure that would enable the question of the relation between syntactic representation and phonological representation to be posed at both the word level and the phrase level. This version was circulated informally and has been cited in other works (see, for example, Allen (1978), Lapointe (1980a,b), Lieber (1980), and Williams (1981a)). Early in 1981, still envisioning this material as a chapter in the book, I substantially revised and expanded the first draft to take into account developments in the understanding of word structure and of syntax that had come about since 1977. I then published the first half of the revised chapter separately as "English Compounding and the Theory of Word Structures" in a volume by T. Hoekstra, H. van der Hulst, and M. Moortgat (Selkirk (1981)).

Not long after making the revisions, I decided that space considerations discouraged including the chapter in *Phonology and Syntax,* and I undertook to publish it separately. It was accepted for publication in the *Linguistic Inquiry* Monograph Series. In preparing it for publication in this form, I have made a few further revisions, with the aim of improving the exposition somewhat. None of the changes is substantive.

As for *Phonology and Syntax,* it is still forthcoming. Its treatment of the word-structure/sound-structure relation relies on this monograph.

I would like to acknowledge here my indebtedness to a number of colleagues whose comments and criticisms have aided me in my work: Margaret Allen, Mark Aronoff, Joan Bresnan, Mary Clark, François

Dell, Irene Heim, Roger Higgins, Steven Lapointe, Rochelle Lieber, Tom Roeper, and Edwin Williams. They have contributed a great deal to the quality of this piece of work, but have no responsibility for its deficiencies. Indeed, had I heeded all of their constructive suggestions, this monograph would doubtless be a better one. But it would also have been longer in the making.

The Syntax of Words

Chapter 1
A General Theory of Word Structure

Within the context of generative grammar, a variety of approaches to morphology have been pursued. In the first work on the topic, Lees (1960) proposed that complex words—compound words as well as those involving derivational or inflectional affixation—be derived through the operation of syntactic transformations from deep structures including only noncomplex words. Chomsky (1970) presented important arguments against this approach to derivational morphology, concluding that derivationally complex words must be present in deep structure. The same sorts of arguments lead one to conclude that compounds are present in deep structure (cf. Allen (1978)). In this monograph, as in other generative works on morphology (Dell (1970, 1979), Halle (1973), Jackendoff (1975), Siegel (1974), Aronoff (1976), Allen (1978), Lapointe (1980a), Strauss (1979a,b), Williams (1981a), Lieber (1980)), the conclusion that words with derivational morphology and compound words are not formed by syntactic transformation is taken as a point of departure. Along with this view, I adopt the somewhat less universally held assumption that inflectional affixation is not accomplished by syntactic transformation, but that, with derivational affixation and compounding, it instead forms part of a morphological component of grammar.[1]

My purpose is to examine what I will call the *syntax of words*, by which I mean the *structure of words* and the *system of rules* for generating that structure. While much has been said in the recent linguistic tradition about the syntactic structures of which words form the basic units, considerably less attention has been paid to the structure of the words themselves. Perhaps this has come about because word structure seemed perfectly obvious, apparently a mere extension of syntactic structure. This is the view of word structure implicit in Chomsky and

Halle (1968; hereafter SPE), for example, and one that is adopted in most subsequent works. However, it is an error to view word structure as merely the "lower" portion of a syntactic representation that is entirely homogeneous in character. It can be argued that, aside from the category Word itself, the categories involved in word structure are distinct from those of syntactic structure and, moreover, that the two types of structure combine these categories in significantly different ways. It in fact seems possible to construe word structure as an autonomous system. In my view, the category Word lies at the interface in syntactic representation of two varieties of structure, which must be defined by two discrete sets of principles in the grammar.[2] Yet I will argue that word structure has the same general formal properties as syntactic structure and, moreover, that it is generated by the same sort of rule system.[3]

In order to underline this fundamental similarity, I will often employ the terms *W-syntax* and *W-syntactic* rather than the terms *morphology* and *morphological* in speaking of the structure of words. The terms *syntax* and *syntactic* will be reserved for their normal usage, though it may be convenient from time to time, for reasons of contrast, to employ the terms *S-syntax* and *S-syntactic* instead.[4]

First, I will argue that, just as it is the appropriate formal device for generating syntactic structures, a context-free grammar is appropriate for characterizing the notion "possible word structure of L." Second, I will show that certain fundamental notions of the so-called $\overline{\text{X}}$ theory of phrase structure (i.e., S-structure) can be profitably extended to the theory of W-structure.[5] As for the question of whether transformations have a role to play in the grammar of words (mapping one W-structure into another), I consider it open. The phenomena I will be examining give no support to the notion that transformations form part of the W-syntactic component of grammar.

A caveat may be in order here. It should be understood that my arguments concerning the formal properties of word structure and word structure rules are founded in large part on the W-syntax of English and related languages. It is enough to consider the Semitic system of derivational morphology, for example, to understand that a context-free grammar such as that of English is but one of perhaps a variety of types made available by universal grammar. McCarthy (1979, 1981) has shown that the characterization of the derived verb forms in Semitic requires a simultaneous "three-dimensional" representation of morphemes. The segments of a morpheme on one "tier" (e.g., the consonants of the verb root) are intercalated with the segments of a morpheme on another (e.g., the "vocalization") by means of their common association with a template, which is a morpheme on a third tier. Semitic derived verb forms thus have no immediate constituent structure. Semitic words also include affixation of the more conventional sort, which can be described in the same way as affixation in other languages. The W-syntax of the Semitic languages, then, includes two components, only one of which is of the sort I am attempting to characterize here. It therefore seems that the context-free grammar theory of word structure I will be defending here forms part of a typology of word structure systems. The substantive claim that I am making is that English word structure can be properly characterized solely in terms of a context-free grammar.

1.1. A Context-Free Grammar for Words

As a context-free constituent structure grammar, word structure rules assign a labeled tree (a structural description) to every word of the language. This sort of grammar thus captures the intuition of native speakers of English (and other languages) that words have an internal constituent structure, the constituents of which may be assigned to different categories. A context-free rewriting system also allows for the recursiveness or self-embedding evidenced by morphological structure; it embodies the claim, a correct one, that there is no principled upper bound on the length of words.

Part of the interest of the claim that English word structures (involving both compounding and affixation) are generated by, and only by, a context-free rewriting system is its controversiality in the current context. Roeper and Siegel (1978), for example, have proposed that a set of what they call "lexical transformations" are operative in the generation of verbal compounds. This transformational analysis will be rejected in favor of a rewriting rule account in section 2.3. In addition, treatments of affixation such as those proposed by Allen (1978) or Lieber (1980) have been based on word formation rules which could possibly be viewed as rules of a categorial grammar. A categorial grammar is at best a notational variant of a context-free rewriting grammar. In what follows, I have chosen to couch the formal theory of word formation in the most familiar terms of the latter sort of model, and leave it to others to argue that it should be done otherwise.

A context-free rewriting system by itself is capable of generating all of the words of a language, but only at a certain cost. Members of a certain class of morphemes, the affixes, display idiosyncratic distributional properties. The suffix *-ity,* for example, attaches only to an adjective and with it forms a noun: *obesity* $= {}_N[{}_A[\text{obese}]_A \text{ -ity}]_N$. The suffix *-ify,* on the other hand, always constitutes a verb along with a sister adjective or noun: *codify* $= {}_V[{}_N[\text{code}]_N \text{ -ify}]_V$, *purify* $= {}_V[{}_A[\text{pure}]_A \text{ -ify}]_V$. The most obvious way of capturing these distributional peculiarities within a context-free rewriting system is to introduce each affix directly by a rule specific to it, as in (1.1), which means, in effect, positing a separate rule for every affix of the language:

(1.1) N $\rightarrow$ A *ity*
     V $\rightarrow$ N *ify*
     V $\rightarrow$ A *ify*

(Such a rule system would also involve rules rewriting the preterminal categories N, A, V with elements of the terminal vocabulary; e.g., N $\rightarrow$ *code, object, boy,* etc., A $\rightarrow$ *pure, nice,* etc.) This treatment of affixes is inadequate, as we will see in section 3.4, because it fails to assign affixes a categorial status and to capture generalizations about possible word structures in a direct way.[6]

The alternative to this purely context-free generation of word structure that I will defend here is not subject to these same objections. It involves a "mixed" theory of morphology analogous to the *Aspects* model of the syntactic base component. The morphological component is seen as consisting of a set of context-free rewriting rules (the *word structure rules*), which (like the phrase structure rules of the *Aspects* model) do not introduce elements of the terminal string; a list of lexical items, including affixes and other bound forms (the *extended dictionary*); and a *(morpho)lexical insertion transformation.* The word structure rules are roughly of the form (1.2) or (1.3). (The term *Af* is a temporary expedient.)

(1.2) a. P $\rightarrow$ φ Q Af Ψ   (1.3) a. P $\rightarrow$ Δ
     b. P $\rightarrow$ φ Af Q Ψ   b. Q $\rightarrow$ Δ
     c. P $\rightarrow$ φ Q R Ψ   c. R $\rightarrow$ Δ

        where P, Q, R stand for individual category symbols, φ and Ψ are variables over category symbols (including Af), and Δ is the "dummy" symbol (cf. Chomsky (1965))

Such a rule system generates labeled trees with terminal strings consisting of dummy elements.

The extended dictionary lists all of the lexical items of the language, including the affixes. The (morpho)lexical insertion transformation completes the structures generated by the rewriting rules by inserting items from the dictionary, subject to the (lexically specified) conditions that the particular items may impose. Among these restricting conditions are the category of the item itself (which must be nondistinct from that of the preterminal category dominating the Δ for which the item substitutes) and its subcategorization frame (the sister category of the item in word structure must be nondistinct from that specified in an item's subcategorization frame).

On this theory, the idiosyncratic properties of an affix are listed as part of its lexical entry. These properties of the affix include:

(1.4) a. Its category (involving a specification of its type (the level Af) and of its categorial features, syntactic and diacritic);

  b. Its subcategorization frame (involving a specification of the category to which the affix may be sister in morphological structure);

  c. Its meaning (usually a characterization of what sort of function it is; cf. section 2.3);

  d. Its phonological representation (minimally, a distinctive feature matrix), as well as a list of its other idiosyncratic phonological properties.

The first two specifications govern the distribution of the affix in morphological structure: an affix morpheme and its dominating category α substitute for a particular affix category β of a tree generated by the word structure rules on condition (i) that α be nondistinct from β and (ii) that the sister of β in that tree satisfy the lexical subcategorization form of the affix morpheme in question. The treatment of affixes here is entirely analogous to the *Aspects* treatment of verbs and their distribution in S-syntactic structure.

This, then, is the model that I propose for the rule system generating word structure. It embodies the claim that morphological structures are labeled trees with possible self-embedding. It also embodies the claim that affixes belong to a morphological category. However, this model implies nothing more specific about the nature of morphological structure. Any further specification of the general properties of morphological structure involves, first, a theory of the categories of morphological structure and, second, a theory of the possible relations between categories in morphological structure.

1.2. $\overline{\text{X}}$ Theory in Word Syntax

Beyond the assertion that the rule system appropriate to generating word structure is a context-free grammar, there is another claim: that certain notions of $\overline{\text{X}}$ theory, a theory of S-structure (cf. Chomsky (1970), Bresnan (1976), Jackendoff (1977)), are required for an insightful characterization of W-structure. We must isolate two basic ideas of $\overline{\text{X}}$ theory. The first is that, formally speaking, a syntactic category is a pair $(n, \{F_i, F_j, ...\})$ consisting of a category *type* or *level* specification n (the number of "bars" of the category) and a feature specification $\{F_i, F_j, ...\}$, where F_i is a syntactic or morphological feature. I will call the feature specification the category *name*. Thus, in $\overline{\text{X}}$ theory, the symbol X (or Y, Z, etc.) is a variable standing for the set of category names Adjective (A), Noun (N), Verb (V), Preposition (P), etc., and the superscript integer (or, equivalently, the number of "bars") defines the level or type of category. The syntactic word is a category of type zero (it is the "lowest" category of syntactic structure). Words of the category Noun, Adjective, Verb, etc., will thus have the category symbol N^0, A^0, V^0, respectively (or, more simply, N, A, V). The class of words itself is designated by the symbol X or X^0 (or some other upper-case letter). Categories of level X^1 and higher are phrases. X^1, for example, is the category level which dominates the head X and its complements, such as a verb and its direct object (e.g., $_{V^1}[_V[\text{devoured}]_V$ [the sandwich]]$_{V^1}$) or a noun and its prepositional complement (e.g., $_{N^1}[_N[\text{facts}]_N$ [[about] [the case]]]$_{N^1}$).

The second basic idea of $\overline{\text{X}}$ theory, intimately related to the first, is that the phrase structures of language conform to certain restrictive patterns, the characterization of which requires the $\overline{\text{X}}$ theory of categories. Specifically, the hypothesis, first put forward by Chomsky (1970), is that phrase structure rules conform in general to a schema such as (1.5):

(1.5) $X^n \rightarrow ... X^{n-1} ...$

That is, every syntactic category dominates a category bearing the same name, but one level down in the $\overline{\text{X}}$ hierarchy. This amounts to the claim that all S-structures have a head.[7] In what follows, I will extend these two basic ideas to the area of W-syntax.

I will defend the claim that W-syntactic (i.e., morphological) categories are entities that are formally identical in character to syntactic categories, which is to say that each morphological category is, formally speaking, a pair $(n, \{F_i, F_j, ...\})$. Note that it is already necessary to view *some* morphological categories as identical to syntactic categories, for the rules of the W-syntax in fact share a set of categories with rules of the syntax—the word-level categories Noun, Verb, Adjective, etc. My hypothesis is simply that all W-syntactic categories, be they of the type Word or "lower" than Word, are in the $\overline{X}$ hierarchy. (It also makes available the possibility that word structure rules may be formulated in terms of these different types.) In principle, it could turn out that Word and only Word is the (recursive) category type at play in language. As we will see, however, a theory permitting only this type is not sufficiently differentiated to allow for the expression of a fair array of linguistic generalizations in various languages, while a limited extension of the theory of morphological category types does provide a means of expressing them. A case can be made, for example, for the existence of a type X^{stem} (where *Stem* is simply a convenient term for the type X^{-1} that is one down in the $\overline{X}$ hierarchy from Word ($= X^0$)) and for seeing Stem as a recursive category type. A case can also be made for a yet lower (recursive) category level X^{root} (or X^{-2}) contained within Stem.[8] The category X^{af} (for *Affix*) is also required, though its position in the system is somewhat special, in that it is not ordered within this hierarchy (it cannot be assigned an integer) and is to all appearances preterminal. (See section 3.4.)

The features which play a role in word syntax (i.e., form part of W-syntactic categories) can be assigned to two classes: (i) the *syntactic category features* [±Noun], [±Verb], etc., which represent the distinctions among Noun, Verb, Adjective, Preposition, Adverb, etc. (cf. Chomsky (1970), Jackendoff (1977)[9]), and (ii) all of the others, which will be termed *diacritic features*. The diacritic features include those relevant to the particulars of inflectional and derivational morphology. The inflectional features might include, for example, conjugation or declension class markers, features for tense (e.g., [±past]), gender (e.g., [±feminine]), person, number, and so on. The derivational features may include ones such as [±latinate] (cf. Aronoff (1976), Williams (1981a)) and [±learnèd] (cf. Dell and Selkirk (1978)). The terms *inflectional* and *derivational* are meant only to provide a loose classification, for the systems of derivational and inflectional morphology are not strictly disjoint. An inflectionally marked element, for example, may serve as the base for derivational processes (cf. Lieber (1980)). Below we will see evidence that the categories of word structure, both pre-terminal and "higher" in the tree, must be specified in terms of features, both diacritic and syntactic. Of particular importance is the claim that such features are associated with affixes, for this amounts to the claim that affixes have a categorial status.

There seem to be severe limitations on the possible relations between the type of dominating category and the types of categories it dominates. First, major constituents of the syntax do not appear within morphological structures generated by the word structure rules. Nouns such as *ne'er-do-well, speak-easy, will-o'-the-wisp*, with apparently syntactic structure, are exceptions and are not representative of general processes of word formation. As for the constituents of compound words which display an apparently syntactic phrasal structure, such as the left-hand constituent of $_N[_N[_A[\text{American}]_A \ _N[\text{history}]_N]_N \ _N[\text{teacher}]_N]_N$, they can be viewed as mere compounds. (There is independent motivation for such a compound structure, as shown below.) Second, a morphological category of a higher level does not seem to appear in structures where it is dominated by a category of a lower level. For example, it does not seem possible to introduce a Word below the level of Root. These observations suggest that word structure rules, unlike phrase structure rules, are required by universal grammar to be of the form (1.6):

(1.6) $X^n \rightarrow \varphi \ Y^m \ \Psi$

      where $0 \geqslant n \geqslant m$

In other words, a category may not be rewritten in terms of another category (or categories) higher than itself in the $\overline{X}$ hierarchy. In what follows, this interestingly restrictive hypothesis concerning the relation of category types in word structure will be assumed.[10]

It is in particular this (putative) characteristic of word syntax—that it is organized into levels (in the sense that a category lower in the hierarchy cannot dominate a higher one)—which distinguishes it from the syntax of sentences. Indeed, in $\overline{X}$ syntax, it is assumed that any nonhead category introduced on the right side of the arrow in a phrase structure rule is necessarily the *maximal projection* of the category (that is, the one having the highest possible level or type specification), so that rewriting rules are of the following form (see, for example, Emonds (1976, chapter 1)):

(1.7) $X^n \rightarrow$ ... Z^m ... X^{n-1} ...   *or* $X^n \rightarrow$ ... X^{n-1} ... Y^m ...

where m is maximal

Should the claim about "level-ordering" in word syntax in fact hold up, then, it would provide important evidence that the systems of word syntax and phrase syntax are truly distinct.

The possible relations between the feature specifications of categories in word structure would also seem to be governed by general principles. For example, like syntactic structures, word structures tend to be "headed" (Williams (1981a)). That is, a W-syntactic constituent X^n with a particular complex of category features will contain a constituent X^m, its head, which also bears those features. Word structure rules thus apparently conform (in general) to the format (1.8), which is to be read as stipulating that each constituent contain a head.

(1.8) $X^n \rightarrow \varphi \, X^m \, \Psi$

where X is a variable standing for a complex of categorial features, both syntactic and diacritic

Taken together, (1.6) and (1.8) amount to the claim that the context-free rewriting rules of any grammar employing such a system conform to the format (1.9) or, put another way, that such a system is capable of generating the word structures of such languages:

(1.9) $X^n \rightarrow \varphi \, X^m \, Y^p \, \Psi$
    $X^n \rightarrow \varphi \, Y^p \, X^m \, \Psi$

where $0 \geqslant n \geqslant m,p$

Of course, this format underdetermines the range of possible morphological structures in a language. One purpose of the following chapters is to show the need for particular statements in grammars concerning which specific categories have what composition in terms of other specific categories. We will see that any given language has a (particular) grammar of word structure (just as it has a particular grammar of phrase structure), one which nonetheless conforms to certain quite general principles governing possible word structures in language. We will see that these particular word structure rules mention all aspects of W-syntactic categories: syntactic features, diacritic features, and category types.[11]

1.3. The Place of Word Structure Rules in the Grammar

In principle, the question of the nature of the rule system that generates word structures is independent of the question of the rules' "location" in the grammar. In an earlier unpublished version of this work, I took the position that word structure rules were part of the system of base rules of the syntactic component. However, this position does not follow in any logical sense from the fact that word structure rules and phrase structure rules have the same general formal properties. It is merely consistent with that fact. Equally consistent would be a model of grammar according to which the word structure rules were "in the lexicon," that is, in an entirely distinct component of the grammar. It is not completely clear to me at this point what this distinction amounts to.

To keep the focus on the issues which I consider to be central here—the issues of the nature of word structure and the rule system for generating it—I will assume, along with the various other generative theories of morphology, that the rules of word structure form part of what one may call the *lexical component* or simply the *lexicon* (understood in a broad sense). As it is viewed here and in most earlier theories, the lexical component contains a variety of subcomponents. First, it contains a list of freely occurring lexical items (which I will assume to be words, in English). We may call this the *dictionary* (or *lexicon,* in the restricted sense). Second, it contains a list of the bound morphemes of the language. This, together with the dictionary proper, I will call the *extended dictionary.* Third, the lexical component includes the set of rules characterizing the possible morphological structures of a language, the *word structure rules* of the present theory. The word structure rules, along with the structures they define, are the central concern of this monograph. Together with the extended dictionary, they form the core of the *word structure component* of the lexicon or, shall we say, the *morphological base.* Other divisions within the morphological subcomponent have been proposed, including allomorphy rules (Aronoff (1976)) and morpholexical rules (Lieber (1980)), but these will not be important in our discussion.

Where this monograph parts company with previous studies on morphology in the generative framework is in its concern for questions of word syntax, and in the explicitness of the proposal concerning the mechanism for generating word structure. With few exceptions,[12] researchers have given little attention to these issues. For the most part, "morphological rules" have been stated relatively haphazardly, with no particular emphasis on the nature of the rules themselves. Presumably the issues were not considered particularly important, though I hope that the reader will judge, with me, that they are in fact significant and well worth pursuing.

One characteristic that distinguishes morphology from syntax, to be sure, is the fact that many of the entities defined as well formed by the rules of morphology are fixed expressions. Most words we speak and understand we have heard before, while sentences are for the most part novel to us. More precisely, what distinguishes words from sentences is that most words are in the dictionary.

There are a number of reasons for saying that the list of items called the dictionary forms part of the speaker's knowledge (or grammar) of a language. First, speakers have intuitions about what is or is not an actual word of the language (as well as intuitions about what constitutes a possible word of the language). Second, and more important, the individual characteristics of words are not always predictable. The meaning of a simple word is totally unpredictable, and even in the case of complex words the meaning often cannot be predicted on the basis of its component parts. The conclusion is that a word and its (idiosyncratic) meaning must be paired in a list; that list is the dictionary. (See Aronoff (1976), who develops this point at length.) Phrases whose meaning is not compositional—that is, those phrases that are usually called *idioms*—will also have to be listed in the lexicon.

Consider now the fact that the multimorphemic words of this list must be said to have an internal structure. Speakers have intuitions about the structure of existing words of their language. These intuitions are presumably based on their knowledge of the word structure rules of the language, and indeed it seems that in general the existing lexical items of a language (more exactly, the words of the lexicon) have structures generable by the morphological component of the language. But the word structure rules cannot be viewed as generating these words anew each time they are used, for this contradicts the notion that they are listed; no distinction would then be drawn between existing and possible (or newly generated) words, and no means would be available for representing their idiosyncratic, noncompositional features. In the case of existing lexical items, then, it would seem appropriate to view the word structure rules as redundancy rules or well-formedness conditions on lexical items. More generally, it seems possible to impose the following condition:

(1.10) For every word of the language, there must exist a *derivation*
        via the word structure rules of the language.

This condition allows us to treat existing words and possible words in
uniform fashion. If a word (existing or possible) is to be well formed, its
structure must be among those generable by the word structure rules of
the language.[13]

Chapter 2
Compounding

Compounds in English are a type of word structure made up of two constituents, each belonging to one of the categories Noun, Adjective, Verb, or Preposition. The compound itself may belong to the category Noun, Verb, or Adjective. My purpose here is not to provide a thoroughgoing description of compounding in English (which the reader can find in Marchand (1969), Adams (1973), and Jespersen (1954)). Rather, I will focus on what I consider to be the essential features of English compounds and their relevance to the theory of word structure outlined previously. In section 2.1, I argue for a simple context-free grammar for generating compound word structures. The important point here is the apparent need for particular rule statements; a general $\overline{\text{X}}$ schema for compounding does not adequately characterize the compounding possibilities found in English. In section 2.2, I take up the issue of the headedness of compounds. The vast majority of English compound types are headed—specifically, right-headed—and the heads of these compounds display the syntactic and semantic characteristics that are expected of heads. There are some compound types which are clearly not headed, however, and I will consider how these should be treated within the theory I am developing. In section 2.3, I present an analysis of the English compounds containing a deverbal head, e.g., *man-eating, timeworn, beekeeper, slum clearance*. I will argue, contra Roeper and Siegel (1978), that such compounds are generated by the quite general set of rewriting rules for compounds, and that their particular privileges of interpretation can be explained in terms of a notion of "satisfaction of argument structure" which already has its motivation in syntactic description (cf. Bresnan (1982b), Kaplan and Bresnan (1982), Williams (1981b)). Finally, in section 2.4, I argue explicitly that the English compound constituent and its component constituents are of the category type Word (i.e., X or X^0). In earlier sections this type (or level) analysis is simply assumed. (This category type analysis of English compounds is at variance with what I proposed in an earlier, unpublished version of this work and in references to it. The reasons for this modification will be made clear in section 2.4.)

All in all, the syntax of compounding appears to be quite straightforward. The rules for generating compounds are banal in their simplicity, when viewed as rewriting rules of the conventional sort. The basic semantics of compounds I also take to be extremely simple (cf. sections 2.2.2, 2.3). I do not profess to have examined this matter in depth, however. What remains to be understood is the role of certain "subgeneralizations" in compound interpretation, such as those outlined by Adams (1973) and Levi (1978), for example (again, see section 2.2.2).

2.1. The Structure of Compounds

As we see from examples (2.1)–(2.3), a compound noun may consist of a noun, adjective, preposition, or verb on the left and a noun on the right, a compound adjective may consist of a noun, adjective, or preposition followed by an adjective, and a compound verb may consist of a preposition followed by a verb:

(2.1) *Nouns*

a. *N N*	b. *A N*	c. *P N*	d. *V N*
apron string	high school	overdose	swearword
sunshine	smallpox	underdog	whetstone
mill wheel	sharpshooter	outbuilding	scrubwoman
hubcap	well-wisher	uprising	rattlesnake
living room		onlooker	
fighter bomber		afterthought	
tongue-lashing		uptown	
teacher training		inland	
schoolteacher			
bull's-eye			

(2.2) *Adjectives*

a. *N A*	b. *A A*	c. *P A*	d. *(V A)*
headstrong	icy cold	overwide	None[1]
honey-sweet	white-hot	overabundant	
skin-deep	worldly-wise	underripe	
nationwide	easygoing	ingrown	
seafaring	hardworking	underprivileged	
mind-boggling	highborn	above-mentioned	
earthbound	widespread		
heartbroken	farfetched		

(2.3) *Verbs*

a. *(N V)*	b. *(A V)*	c. *P V*	d. *(V V)*
None	None	outlive	None
		overdo	
		underfeed	
		offset	
		uproot	
		overstep	

More complex structures are possible as well, since compounding is in principle recursive. Consider, for example, the noun–noun compounds *bathroom* and *towel rack*. Together these can form a noun–noun compound, (2.4a), which can itself appear as part of a noun–noun compound, (2.4b), which in turn may appear as part of a noun–noun compound, (2.4c), and so on.

(2.4) a. $_N[_N[_N[\text{bath}]_N \,_N[\text{room}]_N]_N \,_N[_N[\text{towel}]_N \,_N[\text{rack}]_N]_N]_N$

b. $_N[_N[_N[_N[\text{bath}]_N \,_N[\text{room}]_N]_N \,_N[_N[\text{towel}]_N \,_N[\text{rack}]_N]_N]_N \,_N[\text{designer}]_N]_N$

c. $_N[_N[_N[_N[_N[\text{bath}]_N \,_N[\text{room}]_N]_N \,_N[_N[\text{towel}]_N \,_N[\text{rack}]_N]_N]_N$
$_N[\text{designer}]_N]_N \,_N[\text{training}]_N]_N$

A context-free word structure rule of the form N $\rightarrow$ N N is clearly capable of generating the compounds of (2.1a) and (2.4); being recursive, it generates the proper strings, and it assigns them the correct structure. My claim is that all of the compounds of types (2.1)–(2.3) in English are generated by a system of word structure rules such as this, that is, that the grammar of compounding in English consists simply of a set of context-free rewriting rules. Specifically, I am claiming that the compound types of (2.1)–(2.3) are generated by the following set of rewriting rules:

(2.5)

$$N \rightarrow \begin{Bmatrix} N \\ A \\ V \\ P \end{Bmatrix} N$$

$$A \rightarrow \begin{Bmatrix} N \\ A \\ P \end{Bmatrix} A$$

$$V \rightarrow P \ V$$

As we will see in section 2.3, a simple set of interpretive principles assigns the proper semantic interpretations to the various compound types.

The sort of compounding in (2.1)–(2.3) could be referred to as *native* compounding, to distinguish it from the sort of compounding of (in part) Greek origin, which is common in specialized, sometimes learnèd terminology: *telescope, metamorphosis, erythrocyte, kilometer.* Such compounding forms a discrete system and will be discussed in section 3.4.

The paradigms of compound types given in (2.1)–(2.3) contain several gaps. Among the missing are compound verbs and adjectives whose left-hand member is a verb: $_V[V \ V]_V$, $_A[V \ A]_A$. These simply do not exist in English. By contrast, the compound noun type $_N[V \ N]_N$ is attested, though rare, e.g., *swearword, scrubwoman.*[2] Also missing from the paradigms (2.1)–(2.3) are the verb compound types $_V[N \ V]_V$ and $_V[A \ N]_V$. Indeed, this arrangement of the facts implies that the only verb-on-the-right verb compound type of English is the one consisting of a preposition plus verb. Admittedly, one might contest the absence of the $_V[N \ V]_V$ and $_V[A \ V]_V$ types from (2.3), for the language does contain verbs which seem to display this structure:

(2.6) *Verbs*

	N V	*A V*
a.	globe-trot	sharpshoot
	stage-manage	dry-clean
	air-condition	
	window-shop	
	mass-produce	

       b. browbeat   new-model
          hand-carry   whitewash
          line-dry   roughcast
          housebreak

Marchand (1969, 58–65) argues, however, that all of these are back-formations, which he terms *pseudocompound verbs,* coined with reference to already existing nominal or adjectival compounds. The words of (2.6), for example, were coined on the basis of those in (2.7):

(2.7) a. *Nouns*
       N N   *A N*
       globe-trotter   sharpshooter
       stage manager   dry cleaning
       air conditioning
       window-shopping
       mass production

      b. *Adjectives*
       N A   *A A*
       browbeaten   new-modeled
       hand-carried   whitewashed
       line-dried   roughcast
       housebroken

If indeed, as Marchand argues, all compound verbs like those in (2.6) presuppose the existence of noun and adjective compounds as lexical items, then such types are to be distinguished in terms of their derivation from the compounds of (2.1)–(2.3), whose existence does not presuppose the existence of compounds of other types. While concurring with Marchand's assessment of verbal compounding in English, Adams (1973, 104–109) gives some examples that appear to suggest a (limited) direct formation (not back-formation) of verb compound types, e.g., *chain-smoke.*[3] However, it is not clear that the sporadic existence of such types, an innovation in English, yet reflects a change in the basic rules for verb compounds in English. Assuming the correctness of Marchand's claim, I have excluded the verb compounds of (2.6) from the paradigms (2.1)–(2.3). These paradigms thus represent the types of compounds that the system of word structure rules generates directly, without recourse to back-formation. Back-formation, however it is to be conceptualized (and formalized), is taken here to be a qualitatively different sort of phenomenon, not part of the strictly generative system of the morphological component, which consists of the word structure rules of the language.

The fact that there exist systematic gaps in the paradigms of compound types in English is of some importance. Insofar as these gaps can be shown to be particular to English and not to follow from universal principles, the grammar of English must encode them. This means in particular that the grammar of compounding must explicitly mention the combinatorial possibilities of categories within the compounds belonging to the different categories Noun, Adjective, and Verb. In other words, the rules of the system must be formulated in terms of specific syntactic category names. (The context-free rewriting system of (2.5) does just this.) It would not be adequate, therefore, to characterize compounding in English with a schema like (2.8).

(2.8) $X \rightarrow Y \ X$

> where X stands for $\{$Word; αNoun, βVerb, ...$\}$ and Y stands for $\{$Word; δNoun, γVerb, ...$\}$

Such a schema overgenerates and fails to encode the gaps which are a systematic feature of the word structure of the language.

The case that the gaps in the English compound paradigms do not follow from universal principles is easily made, for the compound types missing in English do occur in other languages. For example, verb compounds consisting of two verb constituents seem commonplace; they are found in as widely disparate languages as Igbo (Green and Igwe (1963), Igwe and Green (1967), Welmers (1970), Clark (1978)), Tonkawa (Hoijer (1946)), and Southern Paiute (Sapir (1911)). Verb compounds consisting of a head verb plus an "incorporated" noun, presumably not derived via back-formation, are also not uncommon; $_V[V \ N]_V$ compounds of this sort occur in Vietnamese (Thompson (1965)) and Chinese (Newnham (1971)), and $_V[N \ V]_V$ combinations are found in Iroquois, Shoshonean, and elsewhere (Sapir (1911)). This being the case, it must be concluded that a rule system like (2.5), or its equivalent, is needed to express the particular compounding possibilities of English.[4]

In sum, we have seen that a grammar of a language must include some system of rules explicitly demarcating the range of possible compound types of the language (by mentioning specific categories). Moreover, I have claimed that this system of rules may be as restrictive as a context-free grammar. For English, this type of grammar generates exactly the necessary class of strings and associated structural descriptions (that is, it has just the right weak and strong generative capacity). It remains to be shown that such a model of compounding permits the proper characterization of the meaning of compounds, a topic that I will take up in the next section.

I should point out that this model of a grammar of compounds is at variance with early proposals in generative grammar such as that of Lees (1960), who argued that compounds had their source in (a plethora of) underlying sentence structures and were derived by transformation. Allen (1978) has argued effectively against this particular transformational approach to compounds, and I will not reopen the question here. More recently, Roeper and Siegel (1978) have argued that a subset of compounds, those containing deverbal second elements (such as *schoolteacher, teacher training, mind-boggling*), are derived by a "lexical transformation." In section 2.3, I will take issue with their analysis, arguing that the deverbal compounds they describe, as well as all others, are to be generated by the same set of context-free rewriting rules. We may therefore conclude that transformations have no role in English compounding; it is unnecessary to introduce rules of this power into the grammar of compound formation.

2.2. The Headedness of Compounds

2.2.1. The Syntax of Heads

The compounds in paradigms (2.1)–(2.3) are representative examples of the class of compounds that predominates in English: they are endocentric, which is to say that they have a head, and that head is on the right. A few compound types in English do not fall into this general class. It could be argued that there is one endocentric, but left-headed, compound type: the verb–particle collocation (for example, *grow up, step out, sit in*), where the verb on the left is clearly the head. Moreover, there is a small number of compound types that are said to be exocentric, having no head at all. I will consider both of these types in the discussion that follows. For the most part, though, English compounds are right-headed endocentric constructions.

In the general case in syntactic structure, a constituent C_i is said to be the head of a constituent C_j if it satisfies two conditions: it must bear the same syntactic category features as C_j, and its type or level must be "one lower" in the $\overline{X}$ hierarchy than that of C_j. In the configuration $_{VP}[V\ VP]_{VP}$, for example, the daughter V (but not the VP) is the head, for only this element satisfies both conditions. The following definition may be given:

(2.9) In a syntactic configuration

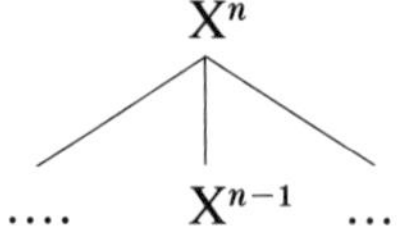

where X stands for some (same) set of category features, X^{n-1} is the *head* of X^n.

Such a definition of head is impossible for compounds, since (i) the members of compounds are of the same level as the parent node (cf. section 2.4) and (ii) both members of a compound may be of the same category as the parent, as in $_N[N\ N]_N$. By what means does a grammar specify which one of these is the head? Williams (1981a) proposes that, for morphology, this be done by a rule, not by the general convention (2.9). Specifically, he proposes the following rule (p. 248):

(2.10) *Right-hand Head Rule (RHR)*

> In morphology we define the head of a morphologically complex word to be the right-hand member of that word.

In word structure, according to Williams, the head is defined in terms of the position of a constituent, not in terms of a relation between categories based on their respective types (i.e., levels) and feature complexes.

As it stands, the RHR is not adequate to characterize the headedness of English word structure, if, as could be argued, verb–particle sequences are left-headed components and if, as will be argued in section 3.3, the head of an inflected word is not the inflectional affix, which in English is on the right. However, a somewhat different formulation of the RHR will cover both these and the right-headed cases:

(2.11) *Right-hand Head Rule (revised)*

> In a word-internal configuration,

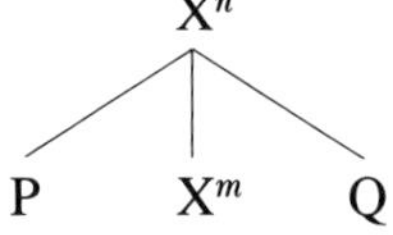

> where X stands for a syntactic feature complex and where Q contains no category with the feature complex X, X^m is the head of X^n.

By this definition, the rightmost category in X^n with the feature complex X will be the head. The definition thus accounts for all of the cases of right-headed compounds, as in (2.1)–(2.3). It also covers the left-headed ones: in these instances, e.g., $_V$[Verb $_{Af}$[-ed]$_{Af}$]$_V$ or $_V$[V P]$_V$, the rightmost category with the same feature complex as the parent is on the left. In what follows, this version of the Right-hand Head Rule will be adopted as a working hypothesis.[5]

It should be pointed out that the Right-hand Head Rule is not universal. As Lieber (1980) has noted, left-headed types predominate in Vietnamese (cf. Thompson (1965)). Left-headed compounds, having the form $_N$[N N]$_N$ or $_N$[N A]$_N$, also occur in French (cf. Grévisse (1969, §291)). (In this case, the head noun bears the plural inflections associated with the compound as a whole: *timbres poste* 'postage stamps', *roses thé* 'tea roses', *bains-marie, chefs-d'oeuvre*.) The RHR must therefore be stated as part of the grammar of English, a parameter which is set for the language.

The head of a constituent plays a crucial role in the description of the distribution of the diacritic features related to both inflectional and derivational morphology. Specifically, a general well-formedness condition on syntactic representation, commonly referred to as *Percolation*, ensures that a constituent and its head have the same feature complex (cf. Williams (1981a)). We may formulate this well-formedness condition as follows:[6]

(2.12) *Percolation*

> If a constituent α is the head of a constituent β, α and β are associated with an identical set of features (syntactic and diacritic).[7]

In syntactic structure, (2.12) ensures that a VP and its head verb bear the same features for tense, for example, or that the case features accorded an NP are identical with those borne by its head noun. In morphological structure, it ensures that a constituent of type Word (or below) has the same features as its head. Thus, as Williams points out, given the RHR and Percolation, the compound structures in (2.13) may be the realizations of the plurals of the compound nouns *apron string* and *Canada goose* and of the past tense forms of the verb compounds *outlive* and *underfeed*.

(2.13) a.

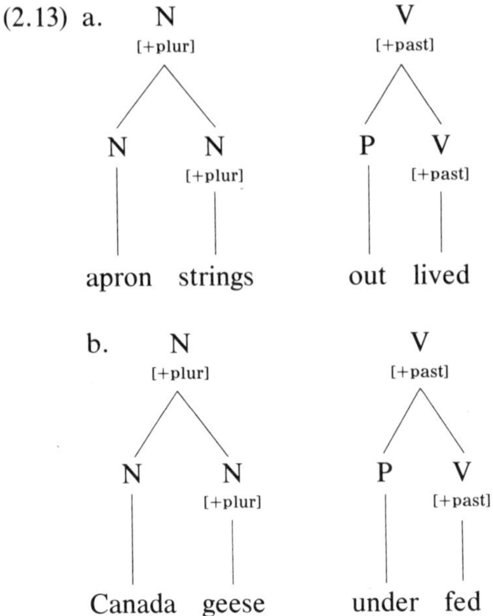

I will argue in section 2.4 that these are indeed appropriate representations of the inflected compounds.

2.2.2. Heads and the Interpretation of Compounds

The notion "head" is crucial in characterizing the semantics of compounds. This emerges quite clearly when we consider $_N$[N N]$_N$ compounds, for example. The compound *apron string* designates a string that is somehow related to an apron, by being attached to one, in the form of one, or whatever. It does not designate an apron that is somehow related to string (or a string). Conversely, *string apron* can only designate an apron which bears some relation to string, a string, or strings. In general, in endocentric compounds, of which *apron string* and *string apron* are examples, the class of elements denoted by the compound is a subset of the class of elements that would be denoted by the head noun on its own.[8] The nonhead constituent of the compound in some way further defines the head; as examination of (2.1)–(2.3) will show, the head is, intuitively speaking, the nucleus of the compound.

The semantic relation obtaining between the head constituent and its sister nonhead constituent can vary considerably, though, and a general characterization of the relation is probably impossible. One important subclass of compounds, which will be termed *verbal com-*

pounds,[9] displays a rather specific and grammatically characterizable range of semantic interpretations.[10] For the rest, however, which I will call *nonverbal compounds,* it would seem that virtually any relation between head and nonhead is possible—within pragmatic limits, of course. This is the position taken by Dowty (1979), Downing (1977), and Allen (1978).

I will use the term *verbal compounds* to designate endocentric adjective or noun compounds whose head adjective or noun (respectively) is morphologically complex, having been derived from a verb, and whose nonhead constituent is interpreted as an argument of the head adjective or noun. By *argument* I mean an element bearing a thematic relation such as Agent, Theme, Goal, Source, Instrument, etc., to the head. (See Jackendoff (1972), Gruber (1965) for discussion of thematic relations.) Example (2.14) provides a sampling of verbal compounds. (The compounds are grouped according to the suffix which, together with a verb base, makes up the head noun or adjective of the compound.)

(2.14) *Nouns*   *Adjectives*

    -er   *-en*
    time-saver   handwoven
    cake baker   timeworn
    schoolteacher   sunbaked

    -ing   *-ing*
    housecleaning   eye-catching
    tin mining   nice-sounding
    well-being   weed-destroying

    -ance   *-ent*
    slum clearance   water-repellent
    surface adherence   germ-resistant

    -(a)tion   *-ive*
    consumer protection   self-destructive
    character assassination   heat-sensitive
    self-deception   *-able*

    -ment   hand washable
    troop deployment   radar detectable
    task assignment   machine readable
    uranium enrichment   teacher trainable

    -al   *-ory*
    property appraisal   disease inhibitory
    trash removal

We see here that in compounds a nonhead constituent may qualify as an argument of the head noun or adjective just as a constituent that is complement to a head noun, adjective, or verb in a phrase structure configuration will qualify as an argument of that head. The semantic relation between *cake* and *baker* in *cake baker* is the same as the relation between *cakes* and *baker* in the phrasal collocation *a baker of cakes: cake(s)* is the Theme of *baker*. The nominal constituent *hand* qualifies as the Instrument of *woven* in the compound *handwoven,* just as it does in *woven by hand. Nice* is an adjective complement both of *sounding* in *nice-sounding* and of *sounds* in the phrase *sounds nice.* And so on. The details of an analysis of verbal compounds will be presented in the following section, where it will be shown by what means the grammar of English, or of any other language, may express the notion that a nonhead constituent of a compound may satisfy an argument of the argument structure of the head constituent.

Only compounds in which a nonhead satisfies an argument of the deverbal head constituent will be termed *verbal compounds.* Thus, the examples of (2.15) are not verbal compounds:

(2.15) party drinker   homegrown
      spring-cleaning   long-suffering
      concert singer   hardworking

The nonheads of these examples add a locative, manner, or temporal specification to the head, but would not be said to bear a thematic relation to, or satisfy the argument structure of, the head. The term *verbal compound,* as I am using it, simply designates a group of compounds classified according to the type of semantic relation that obtains between head and nonhead.

Note next that a deverbal constituent in nonhead position will not have its argument structure satisfied by the head constituent. In the compound *bomber plane,* for example, *plane* can not be interpreted as the "object" (in this case, the Theme) of *bomber* (compare *plane bomber,* which could be taken to mean 'a bomber of planes'). Moreover, I would argue that even in the case of endocentric $_N$[V N]$_N$ compounds like (2.1d) or (2.16), the head noun does not satisfy the argument structure of the verb.

(2.16) hovercraft   playboy   bakehouse
      search party   play dough   think tank
      hangman   punch card   towpath

In a certain number of cases (e.g., *hovercraft, scrubwoman*), it would seem that the head noun is the "subject" (in particular, Agent or Theme) of the verb, yet a fair number exist for which such an interpretation is not available. This is the case with *punch card, think tank, towpath,* for example (cf. Jespersen (1954, VI, 9.3)). This suggests that the former are simply instances where a general interpretation of N in $_N[V\ N]_N$ as something like 'N which has some relation to V-ing' can pragmatically be made somewhat more specific, approaching an argument-like interpretation. In the general case, then, with endocentric constructions like those of (2.16), the verb or deverbal element on the left (in nonhead position) may not satisfy its argument structure with its sister (the head). In this regard, word structure is thus entirely parallel to syntactic structure, where the head of a phrase may have its arguments satisfied by its complement(s), but not vice versa.

For nonverbal compounds, the range of possible semantic relations between the head and nonhead is so broad and ill defined as to defy any attempt to characterize all or even a majority of the cases. (In this observation, I concur with Jespersen's assessment (1954, VI, 1.4).) To be sure, certain subclasses can be discerned. Adams (1973), for example, constructs a taxonomic list of types of semantic relations obtaining between compound members. The following terms identify the classes of nonverbal noun compounds included in the list: Appositional, Associative, Instrumental, Locative, Resemblance, Composition/Form/Contents, Adjective–Noun, Names, Other (Adams, (1973, 61)). But such a list is of little interest from the point of view of grammar. No particular theory or analysis requires a breakdown into exactly these semantic relations or determines that the list could not in principle be extended in any direction. Indeed, many compounds either fit only grudgingly into these classes or do not fit at all.[11] I would argue that it is a mistake to attempt to characterize the grammar of the semantics of nonverbal compounds in any way. (See also Downing (1977) on this matter.) The only compounds whose interpretation appears to be of linguistic interest, in the strict sense, are the verbal compounds, and it is to these that I will turn in section 2.3.

2.2.3. Nonrightheaded Compounds

First, however, let us examine briefly the few cases of exocentric (nonheaded) compounds in English. My proposal is that the nonheaded configurations are generated by the set of rules given in (2.5), but that

they are interpreted by semantic rules specific to them. The first type to
consider is the $_N$[V N]$_N$ compound exemplified in (2.17).

(2.17) cutthroat   pickpocket   scarecrow
       sawbones   cutpurse   daredevil

(Note that these structures are generable by the rewriting rule
N → V N that is needed independently for the endocentric compounds *think tank, scrubwoman,* etc.) In such examples, neither the
right-hand noun nor the verb is the head of the compound and, furthermore, the noun is interpreted as argument to the verb. *Cutthroat*
does not designate a throat, but rather someone who cuts throats. Such
compounds are exocentric, contrary to the general Right-hand Head
Rule. Presumably, the grammar of English will include a statement
specific to this particular configuration, assigning the verb–argument
interpretation to the parts and the appropriate exocentric interpretation
to the whole.

The *bahuvrihi* compounds of (2.18) have been regarded as further
instances of exocentric compounding (cf. Bloomfield (1933)).

(2.18) redhead   hardback   longlegs
       dimwit   straightedge   heavyweight

These structures can also be generated by one of the rules proposed
in (2.5), the rule N → A N, responsible for generating *high school,
sharpshooter,* etc. However, they do not share the semantic properties
of other adjective–noun compounds. In particular, though the adjective and noun are in a modifier–head relation, the noun itself is not
interpreted as the head of the compound, in the sense that the compound does not denote a subset of the entities denoted by the head
noun. A *redhead* is not a head which is red, but rather someone or
something having a red head. These cases will require a rule in the
semantic component of the grammar of English specific to the adjective–noun configuration, allowing for this special interpretation.

Finally, let us look at yet another set of compounds which may be
thought to lack a head. For example, certain English nouns containing
a verb followed by a particle, such as *sit-in, runaway, pushover, speak-
out,* may be considered examples of exocentric constructions, like
cutpurse. There also exist adjectives in English which consist of a
verb–particle sequence, e.g., *worn out, laid off, strung out, tuned in.*
However, if the verb–particle sequences on which these nouns and
adjectives are based are themselves analyzed as (compound) verbs,

then these nouns and adjectives may be analyzed merely as being con-
stituted of such verbs, via a process of *zero-formation* which is quite
general in the language. (Other instances of nouns formed directly from
verbs by zero-formation appear in *her first try, the shivers, a full stop;*
other instances of adjectives formed directly from verb participles are *a
sprained ankle, an undelivered letter, an overturned basket.*) If this is the
correct derivation for these forms, they would not then be instances of
exocentric compounding. The noun *sit-in* would have the structure
(2.19a) and the adjective *worn out* the structure (2.19b).

(2.19) a.   N   b.   A

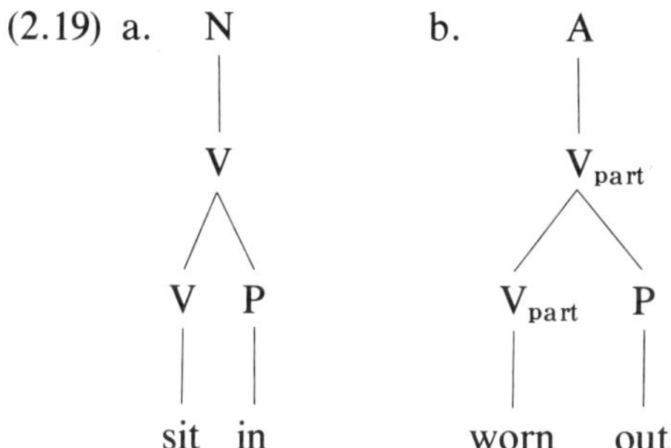

On this account, the existence of nouns and adjectives of this type
would follow from the existence of the rule V → V P and the independently necessary rules N → V and A → V_{part}.

The alternative would be to treat these nouns and adjectives as
exocentric compounds, assigning them the structures $_N[_V[sit]_V \, _P[in]_P]_N$
and $_A[_V[worn]_V \, _P[out]_P]_A$ (generated directly by two additional rewriting
rules, N → V P and A → A P), and to interpret them with some special rules of the semantic component, as was suggested for *cutpurse*.
The crux of the matter is clearly the analysis of the verb–particle combinations themselves. If in fact the grammar may generate them as
compounds, then the first analysis is superior, in that it requires postu-
lating no additional compound rules and indeed predicts the existence
of nouns and adjectives such as *sit-in* and *worn out*.[12]

It is not possible to do full justice here to the issue of the verb–particle constructions in English. Nonetheless, I would like to point out
some potential advantages of the treatment of verb–particle sequences
as compounds. This treatment would involve establishing a relation,
via lexical rule, between compound verbs of the form $_V[V \, P]_V$ and simple verbs appearing in a VP with an intransitive PP (between, for ex-
ample, $_{VP}[_V[_V[look]_V \, _P[up]_P]_V \, _{NP}[the \; number]_{NP}]_{VP}$ and $_{VP}[_V[look]_V \, _{NP}[the$

number]$_{NP}$ $_{PP}$[$_P$[up]$_P$]$_{PP}$]$_{VP}$). With this treatment, the grammar need not allow for a postverbal pre-NP position for PP in verb phrase structure—an advantage, in that only single prepositions (and never full PPs) occupy this position. This analysis would also correctly predict the gapping behavior of verb–particle sequences (cf. Stillings (1975)). Finally, the possibility of "reanalyzing" V $_{PP}$[P NP]$_{PP}$ sequences into $_V$[V P]$_V$ NP, which gives rise to passives such as *Her strange behavior was* talked about *for days* (cf. Bresnan (1982a), Hornstein and Weinberg (1981)), could be explained as being attributable to the independent existence of the $_V$[V P]$_V$ configuration in the grammar. While the details of such a (left-headed) compound analysis of the verb–particle construction remain to be worked out, its aforementioned advantages allow us to see it as a serious candidate. On the basis of these considerations, I will take nouns and adjectives such as *sit-in* and *worn out* to be derived from (compound) verbs such as these.

This concludes our general survey of the role of headedness in English compounds. As has been shown, the vast majority of English compounds are interpreted as headed constructions, consistent with the Right-hand Head Rule proposed by Williams (1981a) and revised here as (2.11). In the following section, I turn to a discussion of verbal compounds, a special class of headed compounds.

2.3. Verbal Compounds

2.3.1. A Nontransformational Account of Verbal Compounds

This discussion will assume that both verbal and nonverbal compounds are generated by the context-free rewriting rules for compounds that were laid out above in (2.5). Examples like those of (2.20a), where the nonhead constituent may be interpreted as an argument of the deverbal head noun, are assigned the same structure as those of (2.20b), where the nonhead bears other than a thematic relation to the head.

(2.20) a. elevator repair   b. elevator man
       churchgoing   elevator napping
       music lover   fighter bomber
       tennis coach   tree snake
       tree eater   tree eater

Note that the compound *tree eater* has been assigned to both sets. This is because it is ambiguous: on one interpretation, a *tree eater* is an eater of trees; on the other, it might denote a creature which habitually eats *in* trees, for example, as in *He was a tree eater by choice and caused his parents great chagrin. An avid eater in the trees, Cosimo refused the smallest bite with his feet on solid ground.* With the latter interpretation, *tree eater* is to be classed as a nonverbal compound. In either case, however, it would have the structure (2.21):

(2.21)

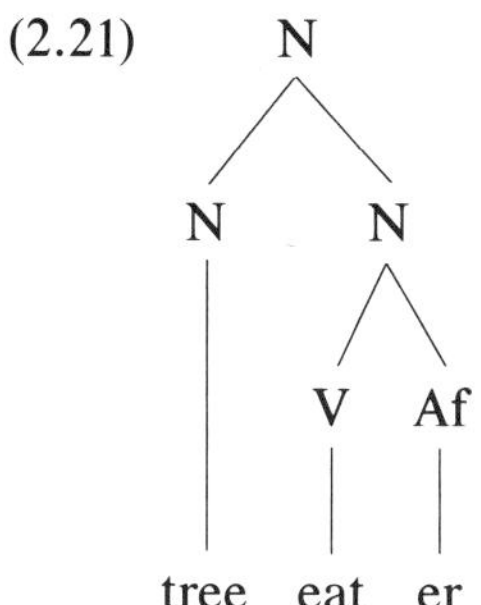

Given the grammar (2.5), this is the only possible analysis available for either interpretation. Because, as has been argued, verb compounds with the composition $_V[\text{N V}]_V$ do not exist, the analysis $_N[_V[_N[\text{tree}]_N\ _V[\text{eat}]_V]_V\ _{Af}[\text{-er}]_{Af}]_N$ is excluded, and because, by hypothesis, the grammar does not allow for tripartite structures of the type $_Z[\text{X Y Af}]_Z$, the remaining alternative $_N[_N[\text{tree}]_N\ _V[\text{eat}]_V\ _{Af}[\text{-er}]_{Af}]_N$ is also excluded. The claim, then, is that the difference between the two instances of *tree eater* is not structural, but only semantic, and that the principles of semantic interpretation in the grammar are such that they allow for both the argument and the nonargument interpretations on the basis of this same structure.

The basic problem in analyzing verbal compounds is to account for the facts that (i) a nonhead may (and in some cases, must) satisfy an argument of the argument structure of a deverbal head noun or adjective in compounds, and (ii) the range of possibilities of interpretation of the nonhead with respect to the deverbal head in compounds is systematically related to the range of possibilities available to the deverbal word for appearing in syntactic configurations where the argument structure may also be satisfied. For example, the fact that *tree eater* is ambiguous, allowing *tree* to be interpreted as either argument (here, the Theme) or nonargument, is to be related to the fact that in phrasal configurations *eater* only optionally requires the presence of a complement satisfying its Theme argument; *an avid eater in the trees* and *Mary's an enthusiastic eater* exist alongside *Mary's an enthusiastic eater of pasta.* Note that *eater* contrasts in this way with the noun *devourer,* which appears to require the presence of a complement satisfying its Theme argument in a syntactic phrase (*?She's an avid devourer* vs. *an avid devourer of trees*) and which, in a compound configuration, requires that its nonhead be interpreted as the Theme argument: in *tree devourer, tree* may not be assigned a locative, or any other, nonargument interpretation.

In developing an analysis of the interpretation of verbal compounds, I will adopt the theoretical framework presented in Bresnan (1982b), which has been given the name *lexical-functional grammar* (LFG). Within this theory, the argument structure of lexical categories plays a crucial role in grammatical description. Williams (1981b) has recently proposed an alternative theory of syntax and morphology which also includes the argument structure of categories as an essential feature of linguistic description, but which differs from that of Bresnan (1982b) in some important respects. Either framework makes available a reasonable treatment of verbal compounds. When the full range of phenomena relating to verbal compounds is considered, however, I believe LFG theory to be superior, and I have therefore adopted that framework here.

I offer this account as an alternative to Roeper and Siegel's transformational analysis of verbal compounds, which I will discuss in section 2.3.3. Many of Roeper and Siegel's insights find their place in my analysis, though the theoretical framework is a rather different one. The point of this exercise is, in part, to demonstrate that a reasonable account of the semantics of verbal compounds can be given within the framework of word syntax that has been developed here, where compound structures are "base-generated." I offer this account more as an "existence proof" than as an attempt at a definitive treatment of this complex area of English morphology. As the reader will see, there are many issues that are left unresolved.

According to the theory of lexical representation developed by Bresnan and others (e.g., Grimshaw (1982), Kaplan and Bresnan (1982)), each word has associated with it a *lexical form.* A lexical form consists of a *predicate argument structure* ("an abstract characterization of those arguments of a semantic predicate that are open to grammatical interpretation" (Bresnan (1979, 100))) and a designation of the *grammatical function* (e.g., subject, object, *to*-object, etc.) that is associated with each argument. The argument structure is the structure of thematic relations for that predicate; in LFG, the arguments are simply identified by number. In this system, (2.22) is the lexical form for the verb *hand,* as it appears in a sentence like *Fred handed a toy to the baby.*

(2.22)   (SUBJ)   (OBJ)   (TO OBJ)
                 | | |
     hand: (Arg 1,   Arg 2,   Arg 3)

(One could conceivably think of (2.22) as being an abbreviation for (2.23),

(2.23)   (SUBJ)   (OBJ)   (TO OBJ)
                 | | |
     hand: (Agent,   Theme,   Goal)

where the particular thematic roles are explicitly spelled out.) The grammatical functions themselves serve in this theory as a crucial link between syntactic structure and argument structure. Grammatical functions are assigned to surface phrase structure positions by *syntactic rules* (for example, the NP daughter of S is specified as SUBJ) and to arguments of predicate argument structure by *lexical rules.* A word with a particular lexical form will be able to appear in a particular sentence structure only if, somewhat loosely speaking, for any argument a which has an associated grammatical function f, there is, in the appropriate domain of that sentence, a syntactic phrase which has been assigned that grammatical function. (See Bresnan (1982b), Kaplan and Bresnan (1982) for details concerning the syntactic structure–predicate argument relation.)

According to the theory proposed by Williams (1981b), grammatical functions have no role to play. On this theory, the lexical representation of a verb like *hand* would include the argument structure (2.24):

(2.24) *hand:* (*Agent,* Theme, Goal)

For any such argument structure, one argument is singled out as the *external argument* (indicated by italics); the others are *internal arguments.* Williams's hypothesis is that the external argument of a lexical item c_i is satisfied in syntactic structure by that phrase C_j of which the maximal phrase C_i having the c_i as its head is predicated. Thus, given that the VP in a sentence is predicated of the subject NP (cf. Williams (1980)), the NP *Fred* in the sentence *Fred handed the toy to the baby* will satisfy the external argument of *hand* (in this case the Agent argument). Williams proposes moreover that the internal arguments are satisfied within the phrase C_i, which is the "maximal projection" of the lexical item c_i. His proposal also involves positing a set of *realization rules* indicating which sorts of syntactic configurations in a language may satisfy which sorts of arguments. Certainly many features of the LFG analysis find their analogues in Williams's theory. The essential difference between them lies in the role of grammatical functions and in the use of the internal/external argument notion. However, I believe that an adequate treatment of verbal compounds is not available within a framework making crucial use of the latter distinction.

To give an account of verbal compounds within an LFG framework, the grammar must presumably be able to assign grammatical functions to the nonhead constituent of compounds. According to LFG, a particular syntactic (or W-syntactic) structure containing a lexical item with a particular argument structure is ruled to be well formed only if there is, in essence, a "match" between the grammatical functions assigned to the syntactic (or W-syntactic) structure and the grammatical functions associated with the lexical item's arguments. But it is not the case in compounds that any particular grammatical function (or functions) is (or are) necessarily assigned to the nonhead position, for, as we have seen, there exist compounds with nonheads having no argument interpretation (and hence no plausible associated grammatical function). For the LFG approach to be viable with compounds, it would have to be the case that a grammatical function is assigned to that nonhead position only optionally. (In this, the nonhead of a compound is quite like the possessive NP within an NP.) The following rule could be stipulated:

(2.25) *Grammatical Functions in Compounds*

> Optionally, in compounds, (i) a nonhead noun may be
> assigned any of the grammatical functions assigned to nominal
> constituents in syntactic structure, and (ii) a nonhead
> adjective may be assigned any of the grammatical functions
> assigned to adjectival constituents in syntactic structure.

(Some analogue to (2.25) would be required in Williams's theory as well. The realization rules would specify that the nonhead of a compound could, optionally, be a realization of any of the arguments of the various types.) Thus, (2.25) would make either the assignment in (2.26a) or no assignment at all as in (2.26b).

(2.26) a. 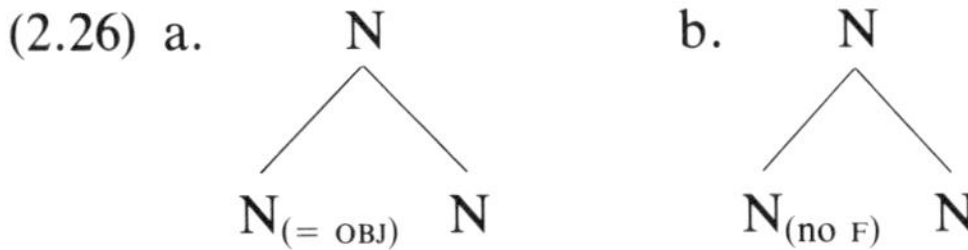

Given the options of (2.26), we can now explain the possibilities of interpretation of *tree eater* or *tree eating* vs. *tree devourer* or *tree devouring*. Given an LFG approach, the lexical forms of the verbs *eat* and *devour* would be (2.27) and (2.28), respectively:

(2.27) 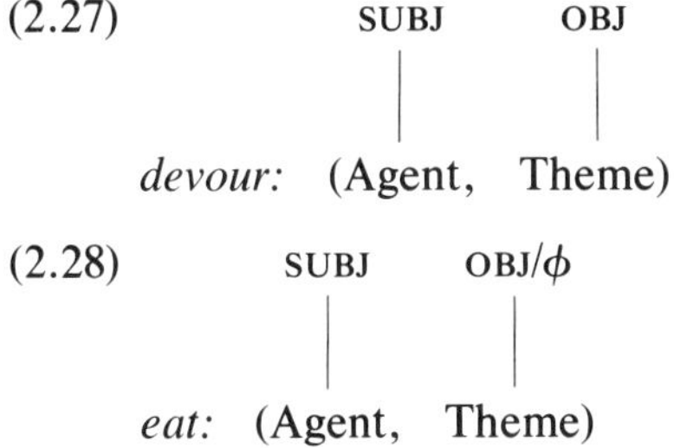

(2.28)

eat: (Agent, Theme)

The designation OBJ/ϕ associated with the Theme argument of *eat* specifies that the Theme of *eat* need only optionally be satisfied by some constituent of syntactic structure. (Compare (2.28) to (2.27).) The derivatives of *eat* (*eating, eater*, etc.) inherit this specification. The derivatives of *devour* inherit the property of requiring the Theme argument to be satisfied by some OBJ of syntactic (or W-syntactic) structure. Thus, the lexical forms for *devouring* and *eating* are as shown in (2.29) and (2.30):

(2.29) 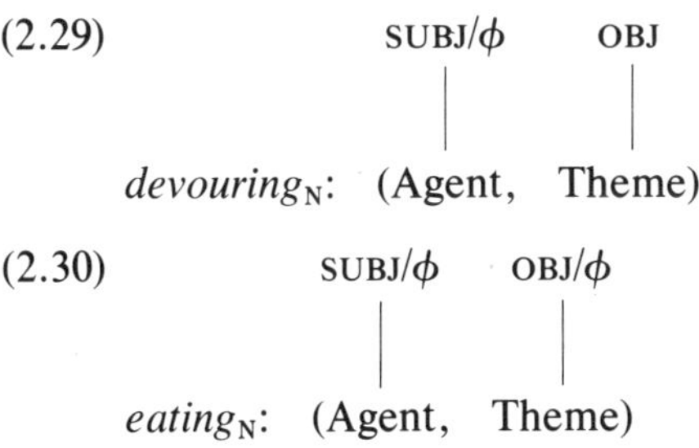

(2.30)

eating$_N$: (Agent, Theme)

Now, suppose that *tree devouring* appears in the compound structure of (2.26a). The match in grammatical functions will allow the Theme argument to be satisfied and the compound to be ruled well formed. If *tree devouring* appears in (2.26b), however, it will be ruled out, for lack of a "match" for its OBJ (even if the S-syntactic structure in which the compound appears contains an NP which is assigned the OBJ function (see below)). Thus, there is no nonverbal compound *tree devouring*. Compare *tree eating*, where *tree* may either have the Theme interpretation or not. I will assume that *tree eating* is assigned the Theme interpretation when (and only when) the compound has the structure (2.26a), and that the nonargument interpretation is possible because (2.26b) is a possible compound structure and because *eating* does not require a constituent to satisfy its Theme argument. Thus, given the different lexical forms of the deverbal heads of compounds, and given the options made available by (2.25), we have the makings of an account of the interpretation of compounds with deverbal heads.

The account is not yet complete, however, for two important generalizations concerning verbal compounds remain to be explained. The first is this:

(2.31) The SUBJ argument of a lexical item may not be satisfied in compound structure.

The correctness of this generalization is shown by the ungrammaticality of (2.32a–c) and by the fact that arguments associated with any other grammatical function *can* be satisfied, as (2.33a–c) illustrate.[13]

(2.32) a. *The hours for [girl swimming] at this pool are quite restricted.
      b. *There's been a lot of [weather changing] around here lately.
      c. *[Kid eating] makes such a mess.

(2.33) a. There's altogether too much [church going] around here.
      b. [Book buying] is on the decline.
      c. Some prefer [gift giving] to [gift receiving].

In (2.32a–c) the interpretation of the nonhead noun as the subject argument (Agent in the case of *eating* or *swimming*, or Theme in the case of *changing*) is not permitted, while in (2.33a–c) the Theme (*reading*, *giving*), Goal (*going*), or Source (*receiving*) arguments associated with nonsubject arguments are perfectly permissible. (The illustration could be made with other types of deverbal elements in head position. Below, in the discussion of compounds containing a passive-participle-based adjective as head, we will see that the Agent argument of the adjective may be satisfied in a compound, but not the Theme argument, since in such cases Theme is associated with SUBJ, while Agent is associated with a nonsubject function (BY OBJ). Compare *mule-drawn* to **plow-*

drawn.) Outside of a compound, of course, that SUBJ-associated argument can certainly be satisfied. In particular, it may be satisfied by a possessive NP within the NP of which the deverbal noun is head:

(2.34) a. I was impressed with the girl's swimming.
       b. The weather's changing delighted us.
       c. The kids' eating makes such a mess.

(The well-formedness of these examples shows that, on an LFG account, it must be possible to associate the grammatical function SUBJ with the possessive NP in syntactic structure.)

Within the theoretical framework proposed by Williams (1981b), no notion "subject argument" can be defined, since grammatical functions are in general not defined. Thus, generalization (2.31) would have to be captured in other terms. This might be done by appealing to the notion "external argument" instead. (An external argument is satisfied by a phrase which for the most part coincides with what would be assigned the grammatical function SUBJ by an LFG analysis.) Thus, (2.31) might be reworded as (2.35).

(2.35) The external argument of a lexical item may not be satisfied in compound structure.

However, this generalization is not correct.[14] On Williams's analysis, the argument structure of nouns in *-ing* must be as follows:

(2.36) *swimming:* $(R,$ Agent$)$
      buying: $(R,$ Agent, Theme$)$
      etc.

The arguments which in LFG theory are *subject* arguments are, crucially, *internal* arguments on Williams's account. This is because (i) these arguments may be satisfied within the syntactic phrase (the NP) which is the maximal projection of the lexical item (the noun) whose argument structure is in question (cf. (34a–c)), and (ii) these arguments may be satisfied by a phrase (the possessive NP) which is not in a relation of predication to the phrase which is a maximal projection of the lexical category. Given this, these arguments cannot be external arguments. (For Williams, the external argument of the *-ing* forms is R, roughly speaking, the referent of the NP.) The arguments in question must thus be internal, but among the internal arguments it is impossible to make a distinction which does not refer to the nature of the arguments themselves (e.g., Agent vs. Theme). And, as the examples above illustrate, this is not the issue—any particular argument *type* (Agent, Theme, etc.) may in principle be associated with the nonhead of a compound. These examples thus show that it is not possible within Williams's framework to formulate the appropriate generalization about the class of arguments which cannot be satisfied in compound structure, and they therefore suggest that the LFG account is to be preferred.

The second generalization regarding compounds is this:

(2.37) All non-SUBJ arguments of the head of a compound *must* be satisfied within the compound immediately dominating the head.

Notice first the impossibility of locutions like (2.38a) or (2.38b), in which the non-SUBJ argument of the deverbal head is not dominated by the compound node immediately dominating the head.

(2.38) a. *tree $\begin{Bmatrix} \text{devouring} \\ \text{eating} \end{Bmatrix}$ of pasta   (pasta = Theme)

b. *pasta tree eater   (pasta = Theme)

This is to say that the structures (2.39a) and (2.39b), which are generated by the grammar as developed so far, are not well formed.

(2.39) a.

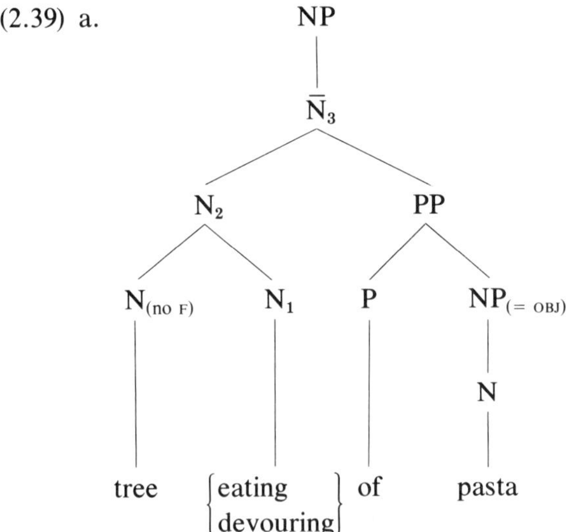

b.

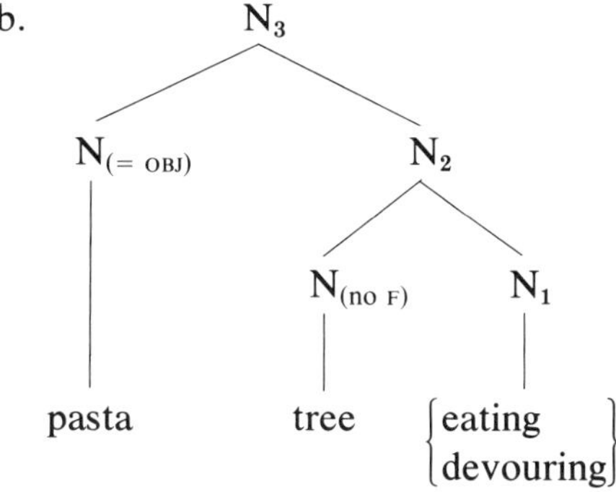

Note that (2.39b) contrasts with *tree pasta eater,* which is well formed, since the argument *pasta* is a sister to the head. The locative *tree* is acceptable in this nonsister position, though we do not as yet have an explanation for this. Another important related fact is that a word having two non-SUBJ arguments cannot appear in a compound. This is illustrated by (2.40a) and (2.40b), which should be compared to (2.40c):

(2.40) a. *toy handing to babies
         *boot putting on the table
         *book giving to children

       b. *baby toy handing
         *table boot putting
         *children book giving

       c. the handing of toys to babies
           the putting of boots on the table
           the giving of books to children

These facts, too, are a reflection of the generalization in (2.37). Any viable theory of compounding must provide a satisfactory explanation for this generalization, as well as for the generalization in (2.31).

It in fact seems appropriate to see these restrictions on compounds as instances of a more general condition on the satisfaction of argument structure within syntactic representation. I will state the condition in (2.41) and suggest that *first order projection* be defined as in (2.42):

(2.41) *The First Order Projection Condition (FOPC)*

       All non-SUBJ arguments of a lexical category X_i must be satisfied within the first order projection of X_i.

(2.42) The *first order projection* (FOP) of a category X_i^n is the
   category X_j^m that immediately dominates X^n in syntactic
   representation (i.e., in either S-syntactic or W-syntactic
   structure).

That is to say, the non-SUBJ arguments of an item must be "locally"
satisfied, indeed, must be sisters to that item. Condition (2.41) correctly
rules out the ungrammatical locutions of (2.38) and (2.40). To see why,
examine (2.39a,b). In each structure, the node labeled N_2 is the FOP of
the noun (*devouring* or *eating*) whose argument structure must be
satisfied, and condition (2.41) excludes the possibility that a constituent
outside of the FOP might satisfy that argument structure. Thus, the
locutions of (2.38) are ungrammatical. The same type of explanation is
available for (2.40a) and (2.40b). When a noun is not part of a compound, however, as in *the eating of pasta in trees* or *the handing of toys
to babies* (2.40c), it is the $\bar{\text{N}}$ immediately dominating the noun which is
the FOP, as in (2.43):

(2.43)

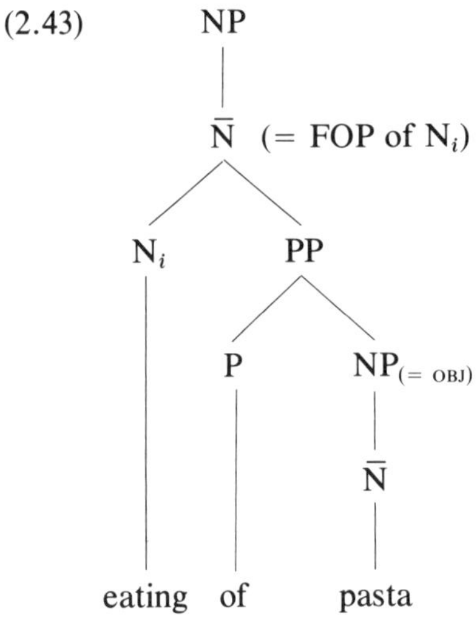

Therefore, the complements to the noun within $\bar{\text{N}}$ may satisfy the arguments of the noun, in accordance with (2.41). The claim made by
(2.41) is a strong one: that all non-SUBJ arguments of a head must be
satisfied by sisters of the head. This is of course reminiscent of the
standard theory claim that a verb, or any other lexical item, subcategorizes only for categories that are sisters to it.[15] It is distinct from, and
stronger than, Williams's claim that the (internal) arguments of a head

are satisfied within the maximal projection (i.e., highest phrase) of which it is head. The FOPC's stronger claim (2.41) appears to be borne out for English, however. This fact, and the fact that the FOPC generalizes to compounds, commends it to us as the proper constraint on the possibilities of satisfaction of argument structure within syntactic representation. In the framework of LFG, we can consider the FOPC to be on a par with the conditions of *functional coherence* and *functional completeness,* which place general constraints on the well-formedness of a syntactic representation with respect to the lexical forms of the individual lexical items comprising the terminal string of that representation (cf. Kaplan and Bresnan (1982)).

This, then, is the theory I propose for interpreting verbal compounds in English. The previous sketch of an approach to verbal compounds shows that an appeal to argument structure makes possible a theory of the relation between verbal compounds and phrasal configurations that does not involve relating these structures transformationally. This theory includes a set of rules (a context-free grammar) specifying the structural or morphological well-formedness of compounds and, disjoint from this, a system of rules for defining the syntactic well-formedness of phrases. The objects generated by these autonomous rule systems have in common the property of being built out of words. These words have the same lexical forms, regardless of whether they appear in word structure or syntactic structure. With their predicate argument structure and associated grammatical functions, they provide the basis of the semantic interpretation of the larger structures containing them, whether syntactic or morphological.

2.3.2. On Deverbal Nouns and Adjectives
The theory presented here holds that the lexical form of the deverbal noun or adjective head of the verbal compound determines the range of interpretations of the verbal compound. Specifically, this theory denies that it is the lexical form (i.e., predicate argument structure and associated grammatical functions) of the verb which is the base of the deverbal noun or adjective that performs this role. In this, the theory adopted here differs crucially from the analysis proposed by Roeper and Siegel (1978). I will consider this point further before turning to a more complete discussion of Roeper and Siegel's theory.

Usually, a very regular relation holds between the lexical form of a verb and the lexical form of an affixed constituent built on the base of that verb. Within an LFG framework, this relation will be represented in the form of a lexical rule or rules. Lexical rules have the power to modify lexical forms, in particular the assignment of grammatical functions to arguments in lexical form. In the general case, the grammar will specify a pairing between a particular affix and a lexical rule or rules. For example, given Bresnan's (1982a) analysis of the active–passive relation, the pairing for the passive participle in *-ed* or *-en* is (2.44).

(2.44) *en*$_{\text{pass}}$: (i) OBJ $\rightarrow$ SUBJ
                (ii) SUBJ $\rightarrow$ BY OBJ/ϕ

That is, the argument associated with the OBJ function in the lexical form of the active verb is associated with SUBJ in the lexical form of the passive participle, the SUBJ argument of the active verb is associated with BY OBJ, or nothing, in the passive participle. This pairing is in a sense the "rule" that expresses the systematic relation between the active and passive forms of verbs. In the context of the theory of morphology being developed here, the pairing of affix and lexical rule(s) is but one part of an affix's lexical representation, which also includes the specification of its category as well as its subcategorization frame (cf. sections 1.2, 3.1). The designation of the lexical rule(s) associated with an affix constitutes, in essence, part of the semantic analysis of the affix. The idea that an operation on lexical forms (i.e., a lexical rule or rules) is associated with the lexical representation of particular affixes was originally put forth by Vergnaud (1973). I have somewhat modified Vergnaud's proposal here, in line with the LFG theory of lexical form.

Interestingly, there are some deverbal forms which, unlike those in *-ing* discussed earlier, do not inherit the lexical form of the verb intact. These cases are crucial to the demonstration that the interpretation of verbal compounds is based on the lexical form of the morphologically derived entity and not on the lexical form of the verb on which it is based. Consider first the case of adjectives in *-able*. While the transitive verb *train* must have the lexical form (2.45),

(2.45)

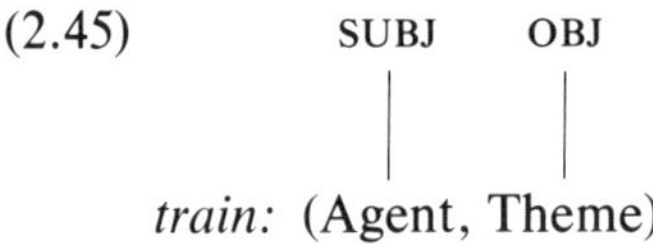

(allowing for *The teachers trained the children,* for example), the lexical form of the *-able* adjective based on it must be (2.46):

(2.46)   BY OBJ/φ   SUBJ

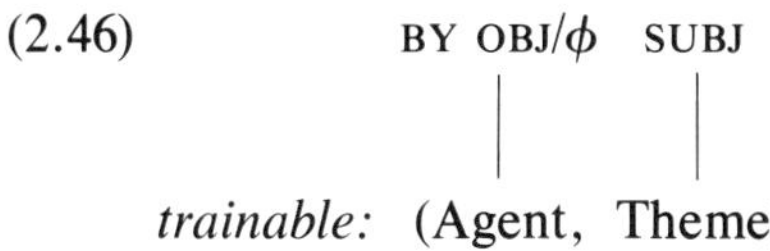

trainable: (Agent, Theme)

(This accounts for the possibility of *The children were trainable by teachers* or *The children were trainable*.) Relating these and other comparable lexical forms is the pair of lexical rules (i) OBJ → SUBJ and (ii) SUBJ → BY OBJ/φ. These are associated with the affix *-able* in its lexical representation.

The verbal compound *teacher trainable* can mean only 'trainable by teachers', where *teacher* receives an Agent interpretation, rather than the logically possible 'able to train teachers', or some such, where *teacher* is interpreted as the Theme. The Agent interpretation is just what is to be expected if it is the lexical form of *trainable* that enters into the interpretation, for it is Agent in this form that is associated with the non-SUBJ argument and may thus be satisfied in a compound. Were the meaning based on the lexical form of the verb *train*, we would obtain the Theme interpretation of *teacher*, given that Theme is the non-SUBJ argument of the verb.

Consider next the case of adjective compounds containing verbal participles on the right side, such as *sun-dried, Aztec-constructed, moth-eaten, slave-built*. Their interpretation is ultimately based on the lexical form of the participle, and not on that of the (active) verb from which it is derived. Our grammar of compounds assigns these compounds the structure ₐ[N A]ₐ. Following Bresnan (1982a), I will assume that an adjective may be based on the passive participle of a verb. The adjective *constructed,* for example, has the structure (2.47):

(2.47) $_A[_{V_{part}} [_V[\text{construct}]_V \ _{Af}[\text{-ed}]_{Af}]_{V_{part}}]_A$

It inherits directly the lexical form of the passive participle, which is therefore (2.48), differing from the lexical form of the active verb *construct* (2.49) in the manner defined by the pairing in (2.44).

(2.48)   BY OBJ/φ   SUBJ

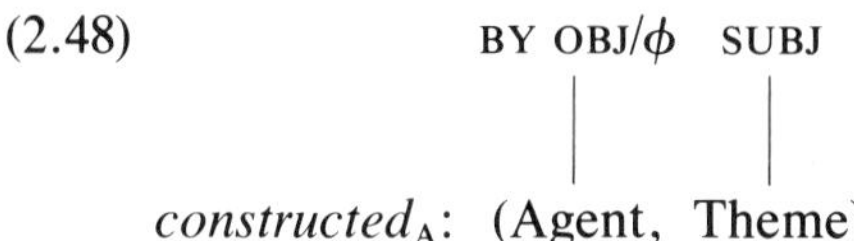

*constructed*ₐ: (Agent, Theme)

(2.49)   SUBJ   OBJ

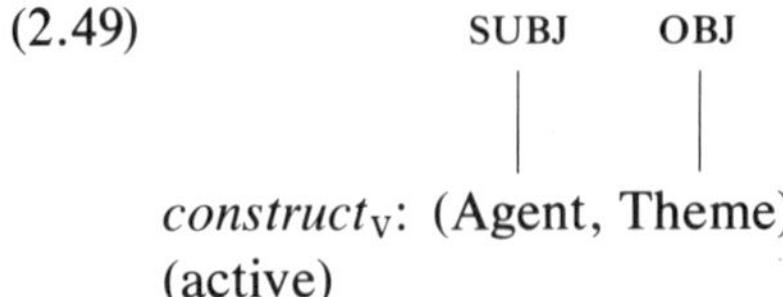

       construct$_V$: (Agent, Theme)
       (active)

It is to be expected that adjectives such as *constructed* enter into non-verbal compounds, since, given their lexical form, there is no non-SUBJ argument which must necessarily be satisfied by a constituent of syntactic representation. And, indeed, examples like those of (2.50) are commonplace:

(2.50)
$$\left\{\begin{array}{l} \text{often} \\ \text{twice} \\ \text{home} \\ \text{factory} \\ \text{winter} \\ \text{well} \end{array}\right\}\text{-constructed shelter}$$

However, as the lexical form predicts, an interpretation corresponding to the non-SUBJ Agent argument is also available:

(2.51)
$$\left\{\begin{array}{l} \text{guerilla} \\ \text{child} \\ \text{Aztec} \end{array}\right\}\text{-constructed shelter}$$

Note, however, that a phrase like **factory-constructed by an underpaid work force* is ungrammatical. This is because, consistent with the FOPC, if a head appearing in a compound has a non-SUBJ argument to be satisfied, it must be satisfied within the compound. More to the point, note that it is impossible to give a Theme interpretation to the nonhead. The compound appearing in the phrase **a shelter-constructed mountainside* meaning 'a mountainside whereupon shelters are constructed (in numbers)' is not well formed, because the Theme of a passive participle, and of the adjective derived from it, is associated with the grammatical function SUBJ. However, if the well-formedness of verbal compounds were determined on the basis of the lexical form of the (active) verb, where Theme is not associated with SUBJ, this deviant interpretation would be predicted (and the well-formed interpretations of (2.51) excluded).

To sum up, the examples discussed here show that it is the lexical form of the deverbal head element that, together with the lexical form of the nonhead, forms the basis of the semantic interpretation of verbal compounds. In other words, the semantics of verbal compounds must be based on word structures like those in (2.52):

(2.52) *Nominal*   *Adjectival*

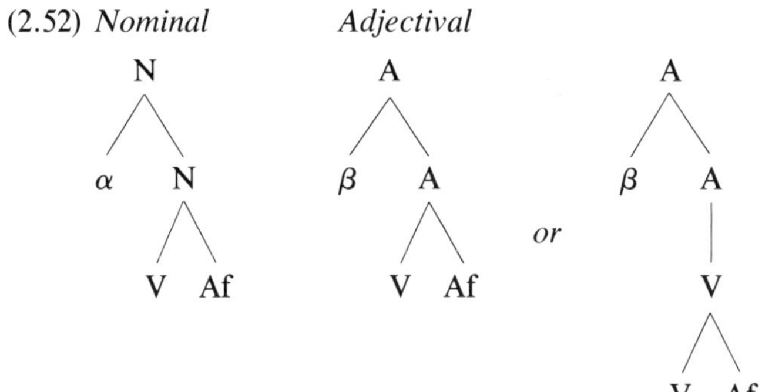

These are exactly the ones predicted by the general theory of the structure (i.e., W-syntax) of compounds proposed here. Such a convergence of evidence, based on both structural and semantic considerations, provides strong support for this theory.

2.3.3. Against a Lexical Transformation for Verbal Compounds

Let us now consider an important alternative theory of verbal compounding, that of Roeper and Siegel (1978). This account has brought to light many extremely interesting facts about verbal compounds, but, as we will see, there are very strong reasons why it cannot be upheld.

Roeper and Siegel base their account of verbal compounds on what they call the *First Sister Principle* (1978, 208):

(2.53) *First Sister Principle (FSP)*

> All verbal compounds are formed by incorporation of a word
> in first sister position of the verb.

(For them, verbal compounds are those ending in *-er/-ing/-en* which have more or less the interpretations that I have described.) The FSP sums up the basic claims underlying their analysis: (i) that it is the properties of the verb (not of a deverbal noun or adjective) that are directly relevant to verbal compounds; (ii) that the syntactic configuration in which the verb appears is related to a morphological configuration (a verbal compound structure) by (transformational) rule, and thus that verbal compounds are not generated as such by a rewriting grammar; (iii) that adjunction of the affixes *-er/-ing/-en* in verbal compounding is part and parcel of the operation in (ii), giving the verb–affix sequence of verbal compounds a source (and structure) distinct from those appearing in nonverbal compounds (which they call *root* compounds); and (iv) that it is the category that is sister to the verb and immediately to its right that corresponds to the category appearing on the left in the verbal compound.

Central to Roeper and Siegel's analysis is the notion that a verb and its subcategorization frame are the source for verbal compounds; that is, they are the structures on the basis of which verbal compounds are generated. Within the Extended Standard Theory, which Roeper and Siegel presuppose, part of the information that is listed in a verb's lexical representation is its subcategorization frame. Thus, the lexical representation of *to clean,* a transitive verb, contains the frame [____ NP]. The mapping from verb plus subcategorization frame that Roeper and Siegel propose involves three essential steps. The first step calls for application of the *Affix rule(s)* (there is one for each of *-er, -ing, -ed*). The *-er* rule is repeated here:

(2.54) (= Roeper and Siegel's (23))

$$[\text{verb}] \ W \Rightarrow {}_N[[\text{empty}] + \text{verb} + \text{-er}]_N \ W$$

It takes as input a verb followed by its subcategorization frame (W) and gives as output a structure labeled Noun which is composed of the sequence [[empty] + verb + -er] and followed by the subcategorization frame. (Roeper and Siegel explicitly claim that the Affix rule(s) are not the source for the affixation of *-er, -ing, -ed* with uncompounded forms, e.g., *loser, losing, lost.*) The second step they call *Subcategorization Insertion:*

(2.55) (= Roeper and Siegel's (28))

$$\overline{\overline{X}}[\text{empty}]_{\overline{\overline{X}}} \Rightarrow {}_X[+\text{word}]_X$$

It involves inserting a lexical item (a word) into an (empty) phrase appearing in a subcategorization frame. The final step is to apply the *Compound Rule:*

(2.56) (= Roeper and Siegel's (20))

$$[[\text{empty}] + \text{verb} + \text{affix}] \ {}_{X_{+N}}[+\text{word}]_{X_{+N}} \ W \Rightarrow$$
$$\quad\quad 1 \quad\quad\quad 2 \quad\quad 3 \quad\quad\quad 4 \quad\quad\quad 5$$
$$[[+\text{word}] + \text{verb} + \text{affix}] \quad W$$
$$\quad\quad 4 \quad\quad\quad 2 \quad\quad\quad 3 \quad \phi \ 5$$

where W ranges over subcategorization frames and X_{+N} stands for lexical categories N, A, Adv.

Example: [[empty] + make + -er] $_N$[coffee]$_N$ W $\Rightarrow$
[[coffee] + make + -er] W

This rule essentially takes the word that (2.55) inserted into the leftmost phrase of the subcategorization frame (i.e., the first sister of the verb) and moves it into the preverbal, compound, position.

A first criticism is that this analysis is inconsistent with the theoretical framework that Roeper and Siegel presuppose: within the (Extended) Standard Theory, subcategorization frames cannot be mapped into syntactic (or morphological) representations. Transformations of the standard variety may map one syntactic representation onto another, and transformations of the type proposed by Vergnaud (1973) may map one subcategorization frame onto another. But syntactic (or morphological) representations and subcategorization frames are, conceptually speaking, objects of quite different kinds (though they share a vocabulary), ones between which no direct mapping can be defined. Moreover, actual words (i.e., lexical items) have no place in subcategorization frames. The theoretical assumptions underlying Roeper and Siegel's analysis therefore need to be more fully elucidated. For the sake of further argument, though, I will assume that it is consistent with the framework in which it is couched.

Roeper and Siegel's analysis has a number of empirical inadequacies that make it untenable. In addition to the serious problems pertaining to the claim I have designated as (i), which have already been discussed, there are others involving claims (ii) and (iii). (See Allen (1978), who advances some of the same sorts of criticisms, and in greater detail.)

One additional problem is that Roeper and Siegel's analysis introduces a systematic redundancy into the description of English morphology. Their claim is that the affixes involved in verbal compounds are generated by a set of rules entirely distinct from those that introduce the same affixes in deverbal nouns and adjectives which do not appear in verbal compounds. Were there only a small set of these affixes, the redundancy would not be so glaring. Roeper and Siegel restrict their attention to verbal compounds whose second member is the agentive affix *-er* (e.g., *pasta eater*), the nominalizing *-ing* (e.g., *pasta eating*), the adjective-creating *-ing* (e.g., *nice-seeming, man-eating (tiger)*), or the passive participle suffix *-en* (e.g., *moth-eaten*). To be sure, verbal compounds with these second elements might be the most commonplace. But the class of verbal compounds is in no way restricted to these, and includes deverbal heads formed with quite a

range of affixes. The list given in (2.14), which included *slum clearance,
character assassination, self-destructive,* and *teacher trainable,* is representative and could be extended considerably. If it is true that verbal
compounds in *-er/-ing/-en* are the most commonplace, it is doubtless
because the formation of (simple) deverbal adjectives and nouns with
these suffixes is far more productive in the language than with their
counterparts in the Latinate system (when such exist), not because
these two types have different sources (structural analyses) in the
grammar. Any treatment of verbal compounds must encompass this full
range of facts. However, given Roeper and Siegel's analysis, the
grammar treats as a coincidence the fact that this rather large set of
affixes that is involved in forming verbal compounds is identical to the
set involved in forming deverbal nouns and adjectives not found in verbal compounds.

This undesirable state of affairs does not arise under the theory of
compounds being defended here. Rather, in this analysis the affixed
forms in verbal compounds are derived in the same way as, and indeed
are given the same structure as, both the affixed forms appearing in
nonverbal compounds and affixed forms not appearing in compounds at
all.

A second shortcoming of Roeper and Siegel's analysis is that, by
treating verbal compounds as structurally (and derivationally) distinct
from nonverbal compounds, it fails to predict that the set of verbal
compounds that are the output of the Compound Rule is identical in
internal categorial composition to the set attested in nonverbal ("root")
compounds. Their system does not predict that the category Verb
should be impossible in the left-hand position of a verbal compound
adjective, e.g., **go starting* (cf. *starts to go*), or that adverbs should be
prohibited from appearing in the left-hand position of a verbal compound noun, e.g., **beautifully dancing* or **beautifully dancer* (cf.
dances beautifully). In their analysis, any constituent type appearing as
the first sister in a subcategorization frame of a verb would in principle
be possible as the first element of a verbal compound. As a result, the
proper restrictions have to be stipulated in the Compound Rule. They
are depicted as having no systematic connection to the array of possibilities independently available in nonverbal compounds.

Again, the compound analysis developed here not only avoids this
undesirable situation, but actually predicts the relevant facts concerning verbal compounds, given that these compounds and all others are
generated by the same system of rewriting rules. The absence of verbs

as a first element in adjective compounds, for example, is characteristic of adjective compounds of all types, both verbal and nonverbal (cf. the rules in (2.5)). Moreover, given my theory, an adjective whose lexical form requires an argument that is satisfied only by a verbal constituent may very well be generated by the context-free grammar in head position of the compound; such compounds will be ruled ill formed on general grounds, however, since the verb needed to the adjective's left will never be generated.

The conclusion is obvious. Roeper and Siegel's transformational analysis of verbal compounds has drawbacks serious enough to make it untenable, while the nontransformational analysis offered above appears to account quite successfully for many properties of verbal compounds, doing so moreover in the framework of an extremely restrictive (and therefore interesting and desirable) general theory of compounds in English.

2.4. The Category Type of English Compounds

In this section I will provide evidence for a number of assumptions underlying the previous arguments in favor of a rewriting grammar of compounding. Recall that the grammar generating English compounds includes the rules of (2.57), repeated from (2.5). It may possibly also include the rule (2.58a) generating verb–particle combinations; otherwise, the rules of (2.58b).

(2.57)
$$N \rightarrow \begin{Bmatrix} N \\ A \\ V \\ P \end{Bmatrix} N$$

$$A \rightarrow \begin{Bmatrix} N \\ A \\ P \end{Bmatrix} A$$

$$V \rightarrow P\ V$$

(2.58) a. $V \rightarrow V\ P$ *or*

    b. $N \rightarrow V\ P$

       $A \rightarrow V\ P$

In arguing for this rule system, I showed that it was necessary to make specific mention of the syntactic category features for Noun, Verb,

Adjective, and Preposition in the grammar, because noun, adjective, and verb compounds do not have identical composition in terms of categories. What I did not give evidence for, but merely assumed, was the level or type of the categories involved. I have been assuming and will now establish, first, that a compound and its constituents are of the same category level and, second, that it is categories of level Word that are involved. (Note that these two assumptions are independent of each other: the compound and its constituents could all be of the same level, but that level could be Stem, for example; alternatively, the compound could be of the level Word, for example, but one of its constituents could be of some other level, say Stem.)

There are two reasons for assuming that a compound and its constituents are of the same category level. First, this assumption predicts the correct array of possible compound structures. The compound category is recursive, as are both of its constituents, and they exhibit the same possibilities of recursion. Consider noun–noun compounds, for example. In positing a rule like $N^n \rightarrow N^n \ N^n$ (when n is a level for the moment left unspecified), we are predicting that a compound may have another compound as its right daughter, or its left daughter, or both, and so on. Examples (2.4a–c) bear out this prediction. The same sort of prediction is also borne out with other types of noun compounds, with verb compounds, and with adjective compounds. Consider the sole case of right-headed verb compounds, and assume them to be generated by the rule $V^n \rightarrow P^m \ V^n$. Because the grammar contains no mechanism for rewriting P^m, this rule predicts recursion only on the right. The prediction is borne out: alongside the compound verbs *undersell, backtrack,* or *overeat,* we can find *outundersell, overbacktrack, outovereat.* There are limits on this right recursion, as shown by the examples *?outoverbacktrack, *?underoutovereat, *overoutundersell,* but it seems likely that these restrictions are stylistic. Structurally speaking, once one degree of right embedding is possible, in principle any degree is permitted—within the sort of grammar proposed here. Turning next to adjectives, it seems quite clear that left embedding is permitted: *bottle green, coke bottle green, ginger ale bottle green,* etc.; *accident prone, car accident prone, motor car accident prone,* etc.; *strange seeming, hard-boiled seeming, motor car accident prone seeming.* Examples with right embedding are certainly less common, but well-formed examples can be constructed. I find the following acceptable: [[collision][shatterproof]], as in *This windshield is guaranteed collision shatterproof but is not guaranteed to resist abrupt changes in air* *pressure or temperature;* [[grocery-shopping][penny-wise]], as in *She's grocery-shopping penny-wise but clothes-shopping extravagant;* [[child-hood][spoonfed]], as in *Being childhood-spoiled and, worse still, child-hood spoonfed reduced Quentin's chances for a well-adjusted adulthood.* Given this evidence, I would conclude that the analysis of compounds as being of the same category type as both internal constituents is well founded.

Further evidence supporting this conclusion is provided by the derivational morphology of English. As we will see in section 3.3, the notion of category level is important in describing the distribution of derivational affixes in English; for every affix, the grammar must specify the level of the category to which it "adjoins." Thus, without yet taking a position on the substantive character of the level, we must say that a suffix like *-hood,* for example, has the subcategorization frame $[N^n \underline{\quad}]$, where n is the particular level and N indicates that *-hood* attaches to nominal constituents. In the most familiar cases, *-hood* attaches to single nouns, as in *neighborhood, sisterhood, sainthood* (there are a number of meanings associated with *-hood*). Interestingly, *-hood* may attach to compound nouns; (2.59) contains a number of well-formed neologisms which I have placed in context:

(2.59) At the beginning, fifteen-year-old Nancy was a confirmed

$$\begin{Bmatrix} \text{pickpocket} \\ \text{runaway} \\ \text{movie buff} \end{Bmatrix} \text{ but the period of her } \begin{Bmatrix} \text{pickpockethood} \\ \text{runawayhood} \\ \text{movie-buff-hood} \end{Bmatrix} \text{ turned}$$

out to be of relatively short duration.

(*Runawayhood* shows that *-hood* must attach to the higher compound node and not to the right-hand member, which in this case is a preposition. A preposition does not accept affixes, nor does *-hood* accept prepositions.) For all of these, we must conclude, structure (2.60) is required:

(2.60)

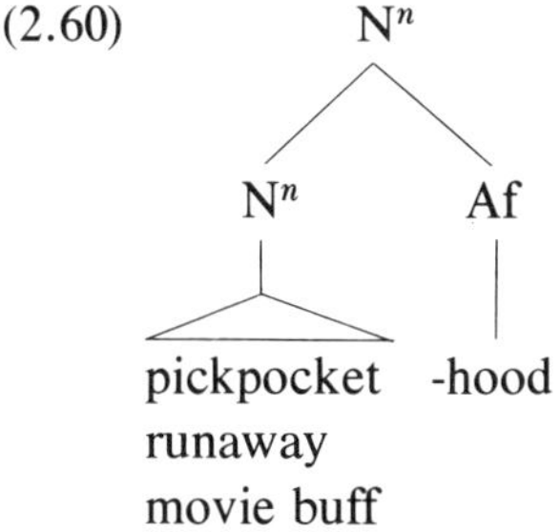

As far as the affix *-hood* is concerned (along with a number of others; see section 3.3), compound nouns and single nouns are on a par—of the same level, so to speak.

Section 3.3 will also establish that the level of the category that is sister to *-hood* and other derivational affixes in English is the same as the level of the category dominating it. This accounts for the higher N^n in (2.60). Given this, along with the claim that a compound and its constituents are of the same level, we expect to find compounds containing constituents which themselves contain the *-hood* affix. And indeed we do:

(2.61)

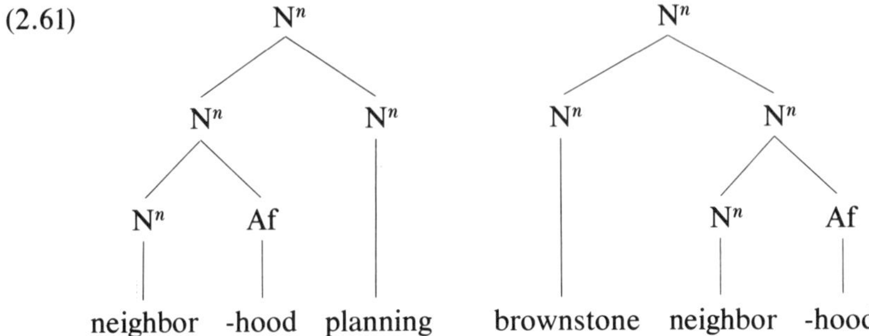

(Note that examples like (2.60) and (2.61), where a derivational affix lies both "inside" and "outside" a compound, are problematic for theories of morphology which separate compounding and affixation into discrete subsystems of grammar. A theory such as the one proposed in Siegel (1974) and developed in Allen (1978) predicts that all derivational and inflectional affixes would be contained *within* compounds, for the rules of affixation (of both types) are claimed to "precede" the rules of compounding. This theory of morphology, which I will discuss further in chapter 3, represents an important alternative to the type of theory I am proposing. Suffice it to say here that examples like (2.60) pose a very serious empirical challenge to Siegel and Allen's theory.)

Next let us determine *which* category type or level is involved in compounding. My claim is that the category type involved in compounding of the sort previously discussed (the native compounds) is Word. This has been assumed in other works dealing with compounds, e.g., SPE and Allen (1978), but it has not been explicitly defended. A plausible alternative to this hypothesis is that the category type involved in native English compounding is "lower" than Word. In an earlier unpublished version of this monograph, I maintained that English compounds were of the level Stem, the name I gave to the next level down from Word in the $\overline{X}$ hierarchy. I now believe this position to be false, for reasons I will review in the paragraphs to follow.

The crucial facts to be considered involve the distribution of the inflectional affixes for number, in the case of nouns, and number and tense, in the case of verbs. Let us suppose that the plural affix *-s* of the noun and the person–number affixes *-ed/-s* of the verb are immediately dominated by a category of the type Word in word structure. This seems to be a fairly uncontroversial assumption, which I will retain throughout. Let us further suppose that there is a category type Stem which is (i) sister to these affixes and daughter to Word, and (ii) the category level at which native compounds may be generated. The rule system (2.62a,b) summarizes these latter assumptions:

(2.62) a. $N \rightarrow N^{stem} \quad \underset{[\alpha\text{plur}]}{Af}$

$\qquad V \rightarrow V^{stem} \quad \underset{\begin{bmatrix}\alpha\text{num}\\ \beta\text{tns}\end{bmatrix}}{Af}$

b. $\quad N^{stem} \rightarrow \begin{Bmatrix} N^{st}\\ A^{st}\\ V^{st}\\ P^{st} \end{Bmatrix} N^{st}$

$\qquad A^{st} \rightarrow \begin{Bmatrix} N^{st}\\ A^{st}\\ P^{st} \end{Bmatrix} A^{st}$

$\qquad V^{st} \rightarrow P^{st}\ V^{st}$

$\qquad V^{st} \rightarrow V^{st}\ P^{st}$

((2.62b) is our grammar of compounding revised according to this new assumption.) However, assumptions (i) and (ii) are open to serious doubt in the case of English. Rule system (2.62a,b) predicts that these particular inflectional affixes will appear only on the extreme right, i.e., "outside of" compounds as in (2.63); it provides no means of generating these affixes "within" compounds, i.e., as part of the left-hand (or right-hand) member.

(2.63)

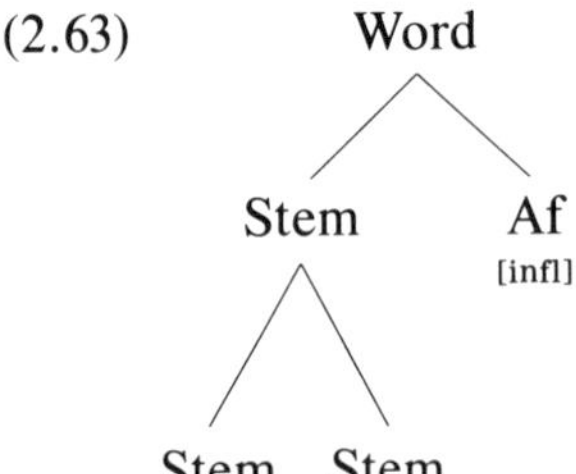

However, this prediction turns out to be false. In particular, there exist a number of compounds whose first member is a plural-affixed noun. Consider the following lists (of which the first was provided by Tom Roeper):

(2.64) a. overseas investor   sales receipt
          parks commissioner   parts distributor
          programs coordinator   arms race
          buildings inspector   private schools catalogue
          home furnishings   tall ships regatta
            department   pants suit
          tryouts judge   human services administration
          arms merchant   high stakes diplomacy
          weapons analysis

      b. arms-conscious   parts-deficient
         sales-oriented   overseas-born
         pants-loving

The internal plural affix that we see here is not the mark of plurality for the entire compound: *parks commissioner* is a singular noun. In these cases, the plural interpretation is restricted to the nonhead constituent. True, many nonhead nouns in compounds carry no plural marker but nonetheless have something like a plural interpretation. In the compounds *dress manufacturer* or *bear trap*, it is not the case that some single dress or bear is concerned; the semantic analysis of compounds must allow for this degree of vagueness. Given this, it would seem that the actual use of the plural marker, as in (2.64), might have the function (pragmatically speaking) of *imposing* the plural interpretation of the nonhead, in the interest of avoiding ambiguity. This is probably the case with *programs coordinator* or *private schools catalogue,* for the corresponding *program coordinator* and *private school catalogue* are easily and perhaps preferentially understood as concerning only one program or private school. The plural may also appear in compounds because, in common usage, it may have a somewhat idiomatic meaning, one that cannot be immediately derived from the meaning of the singular and which the compound must convey. This is doubtless the case with the words *tryouts, parks, human services,* which in their collective interpretation are not merely the plurals of *tryout, park, human service.* At any rate, regardless of the reasons for the existence of such compounds, the important fact is that they do exist—plural affixes do appear within compounds, and this shows the stem analysis of compounds, (2.62b), to be wrong.

It is not particularly noteworthy that examples cannot be provided of compounds with tense-marked verbs in first position, for there is only one compound type aside from the verb–particle collocation that has a verb in first position: the type *scrubwoman,* $_N$[V N]$_N$. In this type, a rare one, no temporal interpretation would seem to be assignable to the verb: [$_V$[scrubbed]$_V$ $_N$[woman]$_N$] is probably ill formed on semantic grounds. As Williams (1981a) points out, the general condition is that inflectional features associated with the nonhead element of a compound must be interpreted (or interpretable) within the scope of the word itself. *Parks commissioner* and other such examples are consistent with this condition. (Note that this condition, appropriately extended, can probably account for the fact that the left-hand members of English compounds are anaphoric islands. Potentially anaphoric elements in nonhead position are never referential, or controlled by some other element of the sentence. The pronouns of *he-goat, she-wolf,* interpreted within the compounds themselves, are reduced to designating gender alone; the morpheme *self* of *self-rule* or *self-conscious* is interpreted merely with respect to the head of the compound (as an object, here) and hence may appear in uncontrolled positions in the sentence, e.g., *Self-rule became a big issue.*)

To sum up, given the assumption that an inflectional affix such as the plural marker is immediately dominated by a category of type Word, along with the facts that (i) a plural-affixed unit appears internal to a compound and (ii) all constituents involved in compounds are of the same level, we are led to the conclusion that (native) compounds in English have the general structure (2.65):

(2.65)   Word

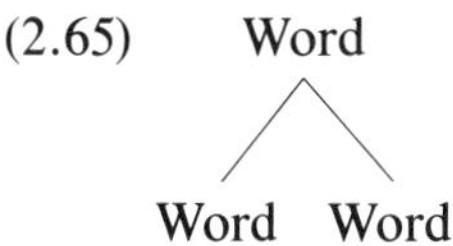

     Word   Word

It is questionable that the rules of (2.62a) are appropriate for inflection in English. An alternative analysis not involving a category type Stem would be the one represented in (2.66):

(2.66) N → N   Af
                [αplur]

        V → V   Af
                $\begin{bmatrix} \alpha\text{plur} \\ \beta\text{tns} \end{bmatrix}$

There is evidence in favor of the latter alternative. It comes from the plurals of noun compounds which are themselves composed of verb plus particle: *pickups, runaways, sit-ins, pushovers,* etc. Whether the internal composition of these is $_N[_V[V\ P]_V]_N$, or simply $_N[V\ P]_N$, the fact is that the rightmost internal constituent is a preposition and thus an element incapable of "bearing" (morphologically) the plural affix.[16] The conclusion is that the affix must be associated with the compound node itself and that the affix must therefore have a word-level category as its sister, as in (2.67).

(2.67)

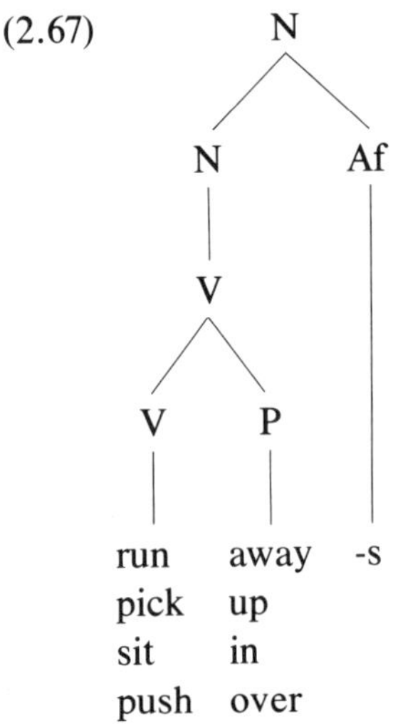

Only the rule system (2.66) in conjunction with (2.57)–(2.58) (and a rule N → V) would allow for the generation of (2.67). (Note that the examples of (2.67) are problematic for Siegel and Allen's "level ordering" theory of morphology, which does not countenance the appearance of inflectional affixes "outside" compounds; we encountered this situation earlier with regard to derivational affixes. See section 3.3 for more discussion.)

The compound rules (2.57)–(2.58) and the inflectional affix rules (2.66) give rise to two possible analyses of noun plurals like *apron strings* and tense-marked verbs like *outdanced:*

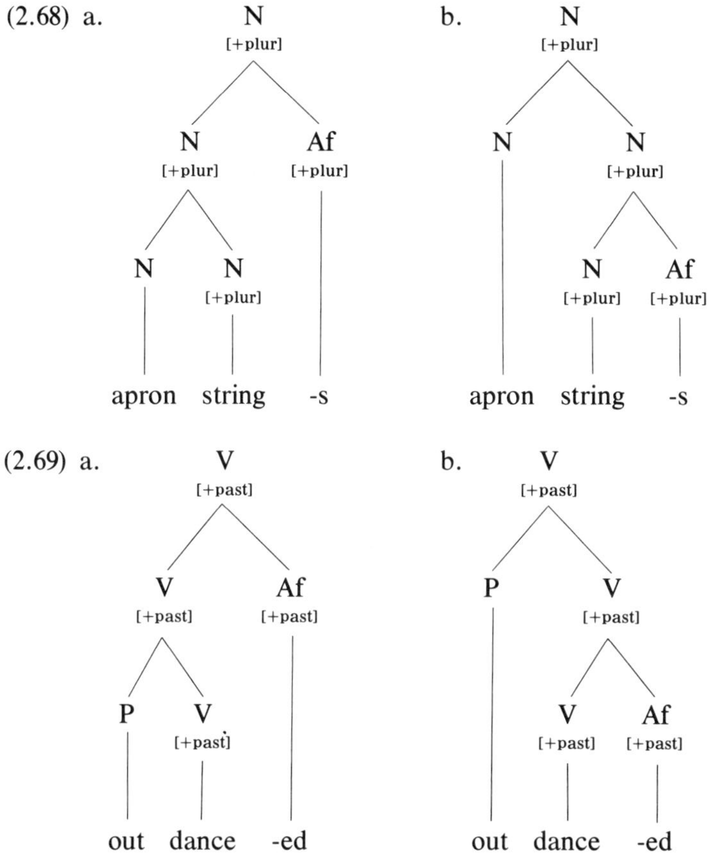

(The full representation is given here, in that the inflectional features associated with the nodes are included. Percolation ensures that the chain of heads will be marked identically for these features. I am assuming that inflectional affixes are *not* the heads of their dominating constituents, contra Williams. I am also assuming that Percolation will have to allow for a limited "summing up" of the features belonging to affixes and the head. See section 3.2 for discussion of this matter.) In the (a) cases, the inflection "marks" the compound as a whole; in the

(b) cases, it "marks" the head of the compound. There is no obvious evidence that the grammar chooses one analysis over the other. Semantically, both alternatives are interpretable, giving the same result. Structurally, i.e., syntactically, both of these possibilities are available, given our independently motivated system. For the moment, then, I will assume that the grammar allows for this systematic ambiguity. Note though that in the case of such compounds as *scrubwomen, Canada geese, field mice, understood, overdid, outran*, where the second constituent is inherently marked for plural or tense, there is no structural ambiguity, for the obvious reason that there is no affix. These simply have the structure shown in (2.70a) or (2.70b).

(2.70) a.

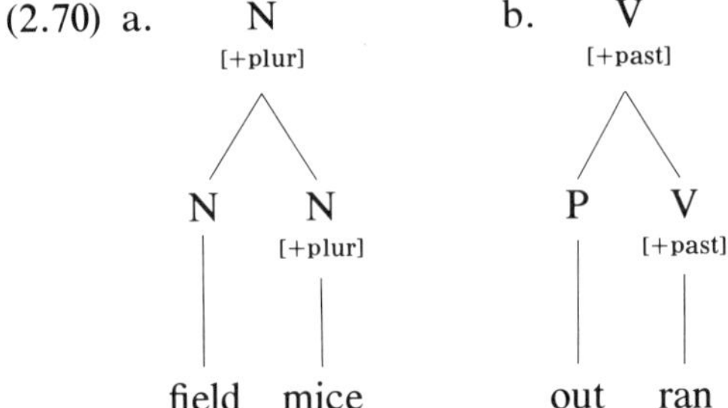

As it has been presented so far, this grammar has one shortcoming. It would seemingly generate multiple inflections, as in the ungrammatical (2.71a) and (2.71b):

(2.71) a.

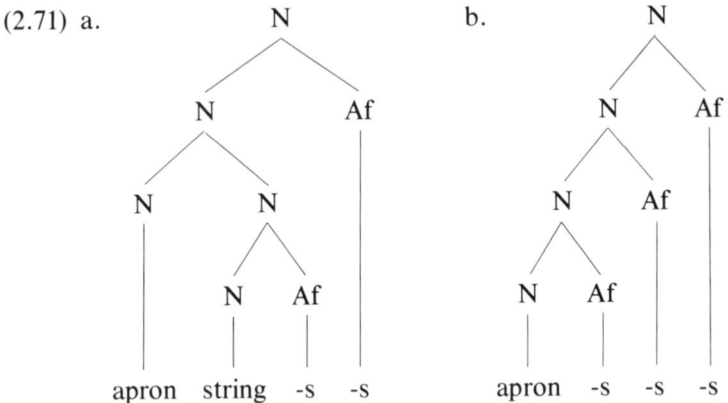

A fairly natural solution in the context of the present theory would be to assign the plural affix a subcategorization for a sister noun that is

unmarked for plural, i.e., [$_N$ _____],[17] and to require that lexical
[u plur]
insertion and Percolation apply cyclically. Insertion of *-s* on the lowest
cycle in (2.71a) and (2.71b), along with cyclic Percolation of the [+plur]
feature originating with it, will result in a plural-marked Noun as sister
to the next higher *-s* affix, one which will hence not satisfy the subcategorization of the plural affix itself. This solution would also rule out the
ungrammatical *Canada geese-s,* where *geese* is inherently [+plur].
Moreover, it would not allow the generation of the compound **field
mouses* (vs. *field mice*) or the simpler form **mouses* (vs. *mice*). Presumably, the existence of the plural-marked lexical item *mice* implies
that *mouse* is marked [−plur] (distinct from [u plur]). The presence of
this feature prevents the insertion of the plural affix, and **field mouses*
is not generated. Note that this solution does not allow us to consider
subcategorization to be a condition on the well-formedness of word
structures. Where we have a well-formed plural-affixed word, as in
(2.68), the affixed noun would have been [u plur] at the point of lexical
insertion on that cycle; but subsequent Percolation will assign [+plur]
to that noun, inasmuch as it is the head of the constituent, and this
would give a "surface violation" of the subcategorization. (See section
3.3.6 for an elaboration of this point.)

To conclude, I have shown that a compound and its internal constituents are all of the same category level or type, and that this type is
the Word.[18] I have also shown that inflectional affixes in English are
sister to a category of type Word, and thus that there is no basis for a
category type (inflectional) Stem in English. The more general conclusion that can be drawn from this description is that the word structure
rules generating compounds are of a different type from those generating phrase structure. The former are all of the general form X → Y X
and thus conform to the quite restrictive theory of possible word
structure rule presented in (1.9). The latter, on the other hand, appear
to conform to a somewhat different schema, that of (1.5). It must be
concluded that syntactic representation is not a homogeneous entity—
words and phrases are objects demanding their own autonomous principles of combination.

Chapter 3
Affixation

In this chapter I will be concerned principally with the theory of affixation. As in the case of compounds, I will focus on the *structure* of derived and inflected words, which in English involve affixation, and on the *system of word structure rules* required for generating them. A central claim is that affixation and compounding form part of the same subsystem of grammar, i.e., that the rules of affixation and the rules of compounding have the same formal properties. The evidence for this claim is that affixes "intermingle" with compounds in the word structures of English; that is, affixes—both derivational and inflectional— are to be found both "inside" and "outside" compounds. Some instances of such structures were illustrated in section 2.4; others will be considered in section 3.3.5. If compounds are indeed generated by a context-free rewriting system, then it follows that affixed forms must be generated in this way, as well. One of my intentions in this chapter, therefore, is to explore the consequences of considering affixed word structures to be generated by such rules, and to move toward characterizing the notion "possible rule of affixation."

In section 3.1 I will present my general approach to a theory of affixation within the framework of a context-free rewriting system. On the basis of this, I will propose the analysis of English derivational morphology that appears in section 3.3. Since it is not my intention to stray far beyond English morphology, the treatment of inflection, which in English is so paltry, will be somewhat limited. Section 3.2 is devoted to sketching this treatment within the general framework. In that section I will examine questions of a rather general order, including the question of the need for word structure rules of affixation to mention category features and the question of the headhood of inflectional affixes. I will also demonstrate the necessity of revising the Percolation Convention to make it somewhat more liberal.

A main theme of this chapter is the claim that a theory of word structure must include a theory of morphological category types along the lines sketched in section 1.2. Such a theory is considerably richer (and hence more powerful) than a theory which might countenance only one morphological category type—Word, for example. Below, I will present arguments that this richness of representation is required in order to capture certain important regularities in the morphological (i.e., distributional) and phonological attributes of words. In section 3.3 I will argue that if two category types, *Word* and *Root,* are posited for English derivational morphology, the various properties of the so-called "neutral" and "nonneutral" affixes can be explained in eminently simple fashion. In section 3.4 I argue as well for a category type *Affix*.

3.1. The Nature of Affixes and Affixation

3.1.1. Affixes as Lexical Items

Any theory of affixation must allow for grammars that represent explicitly and perspicuously the grammatically relevant information that is idiosyncratically associated with a particular affix morpheme. As stated in section 1.1, in the particular model of the morphological component assumed here, an affix is a lexical item; it is assigned to a category and has a lexical entry, like any other unbound morpheme or morphologically complex item, be it a word, a stem, or whatever. On this theory, then, any idiosyncratic information associated with an affix is part of its lexical entry. This information seems to be of three varieties, which I call *syntactic, semantic,* and *phonological,* for reasons that will become clear. I will review how each of these types of information is represented in a lexical entry. In some instances, of course, this will tell us how the affix is to be represented in syntactic, semantic, or phonological representation as well.

A particular affix displays two "syntactic" properties. The first includes the name (*feature bundle*) and type ($\bar{X}$ *level*) of the affix's sister category, and whether the affix is suffixed or prefixed to it. For example, the morpheme *-less* is a suffix and attaches only to a nominal category, of a type to be determined, as in *treeless.* (For the moment, we will assume all of the nonaffix categories in the discussion to be words and therefore that *-less* attaches to a noun.[1]) The second syntactic property of the affix is the name of the category which dominates the affix and its sister. The category dominating *-less,* for example, is always adjectival (i.e., an adjective, given our provisional assumption). We will see in section 3.3.3 that it is in fact unnecessary to state the type of the dominating category of an affix in a grammar of English, since it follows from quite general principles and hence need not be construed as information particular to the affix.

Given the present model, the first property is expressed as the *subcategorization frame* of the affix. For *-less,* this will read [Noun ____], which says simply that for *-less* to appear in a well-formed word structure, its sister must be (nondistinct from) Noun. One could think of this frame either as a condition on the (morpho-)lexical insertion of *-less* or as a well-formedness condition on word structures containing *-less;* however, for reasons given in sections 2.4 and 3.3.6, the former interpretation seems preferable. In principle, the second syntactic property of the affix, which concerns the category of the dominating node, could also be expressed as a contextual feature with a subcategorization frame, but there are reasons to think that this move is unnecessary. Indeed, it would involve an unwarranted extension of a theory of subcategorization frames. As it stands, a subcategorization frame is restricted to including information only about an affix's sister category—not about its mother node or its "nieces" (i.e., its sister's daughters, granddaughters, and so on). As we will see, this restriction can be maintained, in particular because the affix–mother category relation can be explained in other terms.

Following Williams (1981a), I will assume that this second syntactic property involves the categorial makeup of the affix itself. Williams proposes that affixes, like other morphemes, may be assigned syntactic category features; thus, an affix may have the adjectival feature complex [+Noun, +Verb], for example. It is easy to see that, given our model, assigning an affix to a category like A^{af} (which stands for the category pair {Affix; +Noun, +Verb}) will determine, as desired, what sort of node the affix may substitute for in the word structures generated by the rewriting rules. An affix labeled A^{af}, such as *-less,* will substitute for the affix node in (3.1a) but not (3.1b).

(3.1) a. α b. β

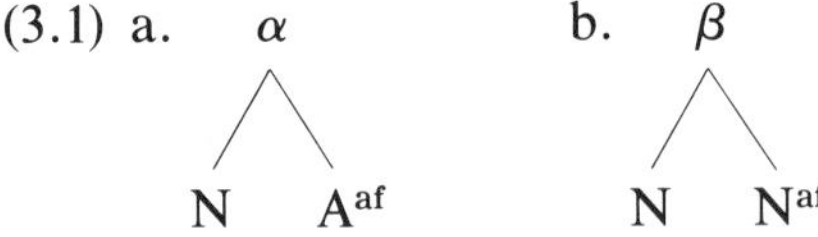

With one additional assumption, we can see that assigning an affix a particular syntactic category may in effect also give information about the syntactic category dominating that affix in word structure. Recall Williams's proposal that word structures (either compounds or affixed structures) are headed. This means that the rewriting system for affixation generates structures in which one of the daughters, either the affix or its sister, bears the same syntactic category features as the dominating category; for example, either $A \rightarrow N\ A^{af}$ or $A \rightarrow N^{af}\ A$ would be a possible rule of this system. Given this assumption regarding the headedness of affixed structures, and given the assumption that affixes have syntactic category features, it follows that when the category of an affix's mother is not the same (in terms of syntactic category features) as the category of its sister, then it must be that the affix is the head; in other words, it must be the case that the affix itself bears the same syntactic category features as the dominating category. Such would be the case with *-less,* which appears in a word structure like that for *treeless:* $_A[_N[\text{tree}]_N \ _{A^{af}}[\text{-less}]_{A^{af}}]_A$. With the assumption of headedness, then, we can see that by assigning *-less* the categorial status A^{af} and the subcategorization frame [Noun _____], the grammar is encoding, albeit indirectly, the information that the category dominating *-less* in a syntactic representation is an adjective. I will adopt Williams's proposal here, for this assumption that affixes can be heads (and that they can bear features) has motivation independent of the present concern, which is to capture the relation between an affix and the syntactic features of its dominating category. (See Williams (1981a) for details of such types of motivation.)

By adopting the theory of headedness in affixed words, we make the prediction that Percolation, the convention regarding the distribution of category features in a syntactic representation, will play a role in such words. And, indeed, it can be shown that the diacritic features associated with affixes, which in this theory are heads, are "induced" on the parent node dominating the affix. Dell and Selkirk (1978), for example, have argued that in French the diacritic [αlearnèd], which is an attribute of morphemes, must be ascribed to the parent node dominating [αlearnèd] affixes: a [+learnèd] affix causes the parent node to become [+learnèd], which has exactly the right results for morphophonemic rules that are sensitive to the presence of this feature in the representation. Similarly, a particular affix may have the property of rendering the (nominal) constituent dominating it [αfeminine], with the result that all words in the sentence agreeing with that constituent will share the feature [αfeminine]. By treating *-ion,* for example, as a [+feminine] head in French, we predict (by Percolation) that *perturbation* is [+feminine] and hence that we will find *la* (f) *perturbation* (f), *aucune* (f) *perturbation* (f), etc.:

(3.2)

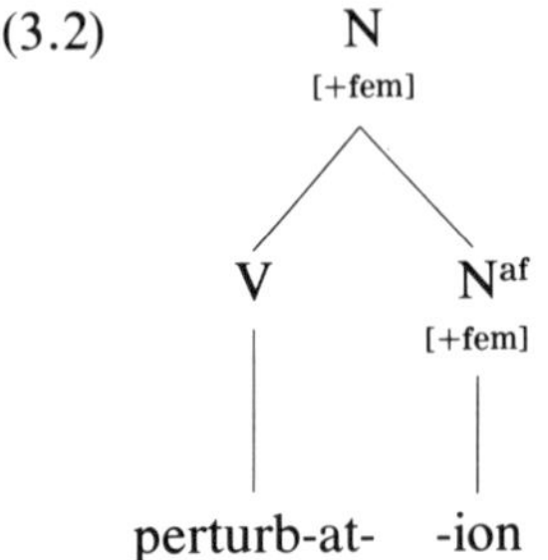

We see, then, that the distribution of diacritic features is correctly described by treating derivational affixes as heads. It is consistent with this approach that the syntactic category features [±Noun, ±Verb] be allowed to form part of the feature complexes of the category Affix, as well. Thus, it is unnecessary in this theory for an affix to subcategorize for its parent node.

Having considered the syntactic properties of affixes, let us examine what I will call their *semantic properties.* In some cases of derivational morphology, the semantic analysis of an affix may simply be a function involving a change in lexical form (i.e., a change in the association of a grammatical function to the predicate argument structure of a lexical item), as in the LFG outlined in Bresnan (1982b). Recall the discussion of the passive participle ending in section 2.3. For such cases, it was proposed that the relevant lexical rule(s) be listed as part of the affix's lexical entry. In other cases of derivational morphology, it may not be possible to characterize the semantics of an affix fully by lexical rule(s). This is true of *-able,* whose semantic analysis involves not only a pair of lexical rules, but also some characterization of the notion "able to be V-ed"; *-able* is a modal operator of some kind. Still other derivational affixes exist for which no lexical rules appear to be relevant. The diminutives *-ette, -let,* etc., are merely modifiers of sorts: in the productive case, the interpretation of N-*ette,* N-*let,* etc., is simply 'small N'. In all of these cases, the appropriate semantic functions can simply be listed as part of the affix's lexical entry. They will play a role in deriving the appropriate semantic representation of the affixed constituent.

For inflectional morphology, the grammar must provide a representation of the fact that verbs containing particular inflectional affixes will be assigned particular interpretations in terms of tense or aspect, for example, or that nouns with particular affixes will be interpreted as referring only to plural entities or to third person human beings, for example. These semantic properties of inflectional affixes have typically been seen as diacritic features of the affixes themselves, and I will follow this practice here. Specifically, the claim is that diacritic inflectional features for tense, number, person, gender, etc., form part of the category to which an affix is assigned, and that these features are semantically interpreted. In the lexical entry of an inflectional affix, these features form part of the specification of the affix's category. Through (morpho-)lexical insertion, an affix will bring its features with it into a particular morphological representation, making them available for semantic interpretation. Note that the theory of feature percolation, which ultimately provides an account of the distribution of affixed forms in morphological and syntactic structure, relies on this conception of inflectional features.

Turning finally to the phonological attributes of affixes, the first and most obvious property to be represented is information concerning the pronunciation of the affix itself. This will include, minimally, a distinctive feature matrix representing the underlying segmental composition of the affix. It may also involve suprasegmental properties of the affix such as the organization of its segments into syllables and possibly feet, or its tonal properties. Other, idiosyncratic phonological properties of an affix may involve its propensity for attracting or repelling main word stress, or its exceptional behavior with respect to certain rules of the segmental phonology. These latter properties may be represented in the form of (exceptional) rule features, which are themselves a type of diacritic feature (see Kenstowicz and Kisseberth (1977)). Also being classed here as an idiosyncratic phonological property of affixes is their phonologically unpredictable effect on the pronunciation of surrounding morphemes; for example, certain affixes trigger certain types of allomorphy in other morphemes (cf. Dell and Selkirk (1978), Aronoff (1976)). As has been argued, this rule-triggering property must also be expressed in the form of diacritic features associated with the affix, in its lexical entry, and in a morphological representation as well.

To sum up, particular affixes, like particular unbound morphemes, display a full range of syntactic, semantic, and phonological properties.

I propose that these be represented in the lexical entry of an affix, falling under these rubrics:

(3.3) *Lexical Entry of an Affix*

    a. Category (including type (always Affix), syntactic category features, and diacritic features)

    b. Subcategorization frame

    c. Semantic functions

    d. Phonological representation

On this theory, the two properties that systematically distinguish affix morphemes from nonaffix morphemes (or morphologically complex lexical items) are, first, the fact that they are always bound (i.e., always have a subcategorization frame) and, second, the fact that they are assigned to the category type Affix (cf. section 3.4). For the rest, affixes are morphemes like any other.

3.1.2. "Affixation"

Given this theory of affixes as lexical items, and the theory of headedness in morphology, the set of context-free rewriting rules for affixation that are included in a morphological component may be limited to those of the form (3.4) or (3.5):

(3.4) a. $X^n \rightarrow \varphi \ Y^m \ X^{af} \ \Psi$

    b. $X^n \rightarrow \varphi \ Y^{af} \ X^m \ \Psi$

    c. $X^n \rightarrow \varphi \ X^m \ Y^{af} \ \Psi$

    d. $X^n \rightarrow \varphi \ X^{af} \ Y^m \ \Psi$

      where $0 \geqslant n \geqslant m$, $n \neq$ af;[2] and φ, Ψ are variables over sequences of category symbols

(3.5) a. $X^m \rightarrow \Delta$

    b. $Y^m \rightarrow \Delta$

      where $0 \geqslant m$, m may $=$ af

It is suggested that languages may choose from among the schemata in (3.4). An entirely suffixing language, for example, would include only rules of the form (3.4a) and/or (3.4c). Another parameter of choice may be whether word structures are binary or multiply branching; this choice is made as a condition on the variables φ and Ψ. For English, it may be argued, φ and Ψ are equal to zero, which is to say that the language has only binary word structures.

One important question is whether or not the word structure rules of a given language need be any more specific than the schemata of (3.4). In other words, are these schemata themselves (or some subset) the word structure rules of a language, or merely the universally specified "templates" to which language-particular rules must conform? In our examination of English compounds, the answer was that language-particular rules, in all their specificity, were required in the grammar. The situation with regard to affixes is less clear, for much of the information about the word structure in which an affix appears (specifically, the names of the sister and mother categories) inheres in the lexical entry of the affix itself. The affix is strictly subcategorized for a sister of a particular category name, and, depending on its position in the W-structure, either its features or its sister's will be in a percolation relation to the mother node. Thus, it is entirely possible to consider that the W-structures generated by the affixation rules contain no category names, but that they acquire them through lexical insertion and percolation. This in fact resembles the position adopted in Lieber (1980). We will see in sections 3.2.2 and 3.3.2, however, that certain language-specific generalizations about W-structure are lost if the word structure rules themselves are not given the power to mention particular features or category names.

The other reason that the schemata in (3.4) are insufficiently specific, of course, is that they do not tell us what category types may be involved in the word structures of particular languages. Information about category types in word structure is only partially contained in an affix's lexical specification and thus cannot be "induced" in the representation from the affix itself. In particular, our theory is that the affix specifies only the category type (and name) of its sister. Thus, the category type of the mother cannot be learned from the affix (nor can it be obtained through percolation, a relation involving only category features). Of course, the theory of affix subcategorization could be modified so as to include such information. However, I resist this move. This is partly because I assume that, in general, the $\overline{X}$ types (levels) that are involved in the (W- or S-) syntactic structure of a language are not specified merely via the lexical representation of the lexical items of the language, but rather that the grammar itself contains some independent statement on this matter. (See section 3.4 and Stowell (1981) for some discussion of this point.) Therefore, I take the position that schemata like (3.4a–d) are indeed a set of universally provided abstract "templates," to which the word structure rule systems of languages will (more or less) conform.

Given a context-free rule system conforming to the schemata of (3.4), then, categories of type Affix, along with categories of type Word, etc., are generated by rule in abstract word structures. Through lexical insertion, particular lexical items (affixes or nonaffixes) substitute for the preterminal categories of these abstract word structures, thereby completing them. Consider for example the English affixation rules (3.6a,b):

(3.6) a. $A \rightarrow N\ A^{af}$
      b. $N \rightarrow A\ N^{af}$

Taken separately, each will generate one of the simple structures of (3.7) (in conjunction with dummy-introducing rules):

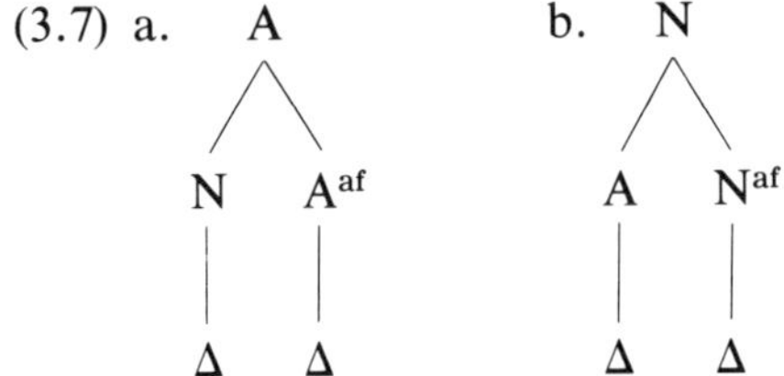

Given a lexicon of English that includes the (partial) entries of (3.8), and given lexical insertion, the structures of (3.7) will yield the words in (3.9).

(3.8) *tree:*   (i) Noun
      sad: (i) Adj
      -ness: (i) Noun^{af}
                 (ii) [Adj ____]
      -less: (i) Adj^{af}
                 (ii) [Noun ____]

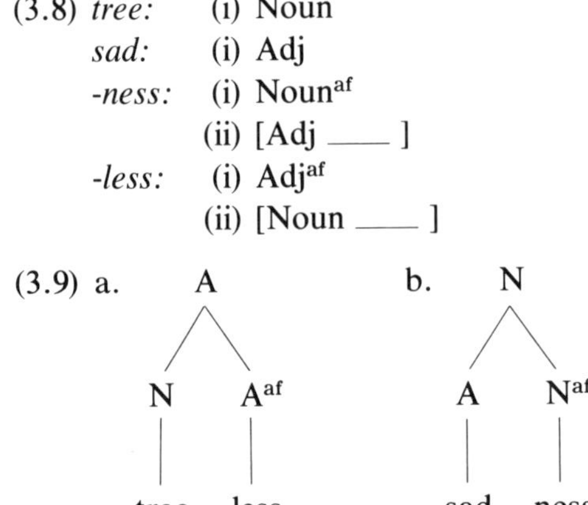

A context-free grammar seems to be quite appropriate as the model of the rule system generating the well-formed affixed word structures of English, just as it seems to be for compounds. With such a model there is no limit on the possible length of the sequence of affixes in words, which is as it should be. The recursiveness of the system can be illustrated by considering the joint effect of just two rules of the grammar, (3.6a,b). Together, these rules generate a set of structures that is unlimited in size, including for example (3.10a–c).

(3.10) a.   b.   c.

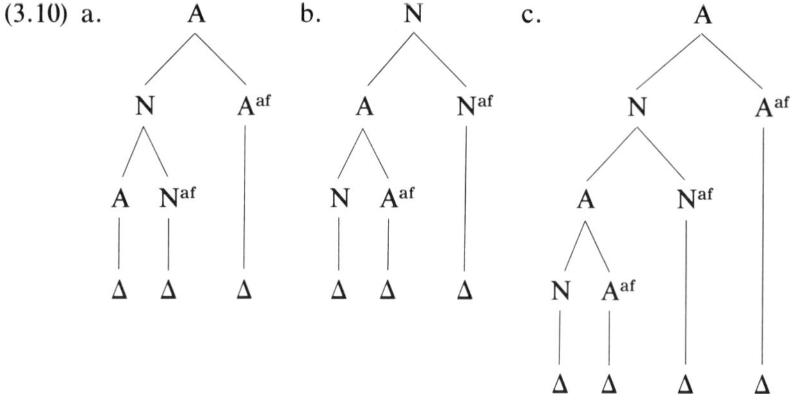

The grammar thus provides for the possibility of generating (assigning a structural description to) words such as $[[[pain]_N$ -ful$]_A$ -ness$]_N$, $[[[tender]_A$ -ness$]_N$ -less$]_A$, $[[[[fool]_N$ -ish$]_A$ -ness$]_N$ -less$]_A$, and potentially even longer ones. A context-free grammar also has the proper strong generative capacity: it assigns the proper structural description (i.e., trees, labeled bracketings) to the strings that it generates. Evidence that a labeled tree representation is necessary for affixed words is provided not only by the intuitions of native speakers concerning the internal structure of words, but also by processes which interpret these structures, be they semantic or phonological. As SPE demonstrated, for instance, the internal structure of a word may determine in part its accentual properties.[3] We see, then, that a rule system with the weak and strong generative capacity of a context-free grammar forms a necessary part of any model of the morphological component of English.

As I mentioned in chapter 1, there is an alternative to the "mixed" model of the morphological component that I have proposed here, one that eliminates the lexical representation of affixes and does away with assigning them a categorial status. This alternative is a context-free grammar whose rules directly introduce the affix morphemes as elements of the terminal string. I have already suggested two apparent drawbacks to this model. First, it removes the possibility of making statements in the grammar regarding the structure of affixed forms in general. For example, with this model, it is not possible (as it is with (3.6)) to express the generalization that in English an adjective may consist of a noun plus a suffix.[4] Without the category Affix, a bevy of word structure rules is required, as in (3.11).

(3.11) A → N *ly*   (*friendly*)
       A → N *ed*   (*talented*)
       A → N *y*   (*grimy*)
       A → N *less*   (*homeless*)
       A → N *ish*   (*loutish*)
       A → N *ful*   (*willful*)
       A → N *able*   (*fashionable*)

Such a rule system is also unable to express the generalization about English word structure that "category-changing" affixes are suffixes. (See section 3.3.2 for some discussion.)

The second drawback is that the word structures generated by this rule system are insufficiently rich: the affix morpheme, which is an element of the terminal string (where I assume this to be the phonological representation), is directly dominated by the category node which also dominates its sister category. Instead of (3.9), the grammar would generate (3.12).

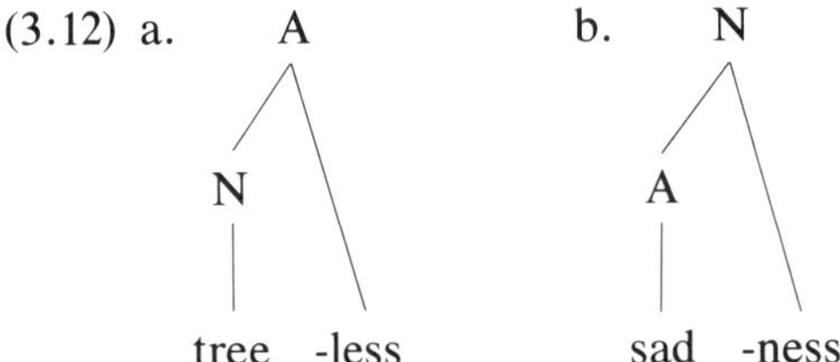

This, we will see, provides an inadequate representation of affixes from the point of view of grammatical processes which apply to morphological structure, as well as those describing affix distribution. Such processes must apparently appeal to the categorial status of affixes—specifically, to their associated feature complexes. In the following sections, I will assume the "mixed" model of the morphological component that I have proposed here; at the same time, when the relevant evidence arises, I will point out the inadequacies of the "pure" context-free grammar approach. I will discuss this issue more fully in section 3.4.

3.2. Inflectional Affixation

3.2.1. Against a Transformational Derivation of Inflection

There is some debate about including inflectional morphology along with derivational morphology and compounding as part of the structure generated by rules of the morphological component. It has been assumed in many works (e.g., SPE, Chomsky (1970), Aronoff (1976), Siegel (1974)) that inflectional morphology is introduced by syntactic transformations. The rule of Affix Hopping in English, proposed by Chomsky (1957), is a classic example of a transformation that participates in the defining of surface word structure. But there are strong reasons for rejecting the notion that inflectional morphology is transformationally derived. First, it is not clear that a principled line can actually be drawn between inflection and derivation. For example, it may not be possible to ascribe an inflectional rather than a derivational status to a given affix on the basis of its semantic function. Moreover, in terms of distribution, inflectionally marked items may appear both inside and outside structures involving compounding (as in English; see section 2.4) or derivational affixes (see Lieber (1980)), where the latter are said to be generated by rules of the morphological component. Moreover, deriving inflected forms via transformations makes it impossible for a grammar to express real generalizations about their shape— the fact that all regular inflection in English is borne by suffixes, for example, or that in some other language all forms of plural suffixes precede all case-marking suffixes in the noun. Each language would exhibit an inexplicable convergence in the effects of inflection-assigning transformations, toward a single canonical pattern within the word. A system of transformational derivation is unable to express this canonical pattern directly, while a system of word structure rules for inflection would be designed to do just that. (Note that this is just the sort of argument made by Chomsky (1972a) for a level of deep structure, characterized by a set of phrase structure rules, and against the Generative Semantics transformational derivation of surface structure, in any language, from a universal underlying logical form.) Finally, a theory according to which transformations adjoin inflectional affixes in making words provides no explanation for the fact that S-syntactic transformations do not appear to perform other sorts of operations on words or parts of words, such as deletion or inversion. Lapointe (1980a,b) argues for what he calls the *Generalized Lexicalist Hypothesis* (GLH)—according to which "No syntactic rule can refer to a morphological feature or category"—making a strong case that some generalization of this sort is part of the theory of language. It follows from the GLH, of course, that inflectional affixes may not be manipulated by S-syntactic transformations. A somewhat weaker condition on the ability of rules to involve both S-structure and W-structure may be in order, however, one that would not prevent rules from analyzing (i.e., examining) W-structure and S-structure in the same structural description, but would exclude structural changes which altered the structures in any way (through movement or deletion). Such a weakening would allow for rules of interpretation which might (for example) establish anaphoric relations between parts of words and elements of S-structure. As an alternative to Lapointe's condition, I propose the following:

(3.13) *The Word Structure Autonomy Condition*

> No deletion or movement transformation may involve
> categories of both W-structure and S-structure.

Even in this rough form, the condition rules out the manipulation of affixes, which are categories of W-structure, by transformations applying on an S-syntactic domain. The condition will doubtless have to be refined, depending, for example, on whether compounds whose constituents are of type Word may be manipulated by S-syntactic transformations. I will not pursue any refinements here. The point is simply that the fact that such a condition seems generally valid suggests very strongly that inflectional affixation is not performed transformationally. On the basis of the foregoing considerations, we must conclude that inflection is as appropriately included in the morphological component as any other sort of word-formation phenomenon.

This approach to inflection does not deny the syntax its proper role in defining the distributional possibilities of inflected items within the sentence; rather, it denies merely that the affixation is performed by the syntax. It is entirely within the power of the rules of syntax—and appropriately so, I believe—to specify that such and such a category (word or phrase) must bear such and such inflectional features when appearing in such and such syntactic configurations.[5] The Percolation Convention will do the rest, ensuring that within a constituent marked in this way, the head word will either itself be inherently specified for the feature(s) or contain an affix (or affixes) in an appropriate configuration within it that is (or are) so specified. This is essentially the approach of Williams (1981a), and it will be assumed here. (See Lapointe (1980a) for a somewhat different proposal for describing the distribution of inflected items in the sentence without appeal to inflectional affixing by transformation.)

My claim, then, is that inflectional affixation is a matter for the rewriting rules of the morphological component. In the following sections, I will consider the issues raised for the general theory of word structure by the rules for inflection and by the inflected structures themselves. There are two main questions to be addressed. First, how specific are word structure rules for inflection? In particular, must they mention specific features? (Recall the discussion in section 3.1.2.) My answer to this question is affirmative. The second question, to be taken up in section 3.2.3, concerns the headedness of inflected structures. Is the verb or its inflectional affix the head of an inflected verb? The answer here, I believe (contra Williams), is that inflectional affixes are *not* heads.

3.2.2. Word Structure Rules for Inflection

I am claiming, then, that inflectional morphology is a matter for the morphological component and, more specifically, that it may be characterized by a set of context-free word structure rules. For English, the rules are apparently just those of (2.66), which I repeat here in somewhat modified form. (The feature specification *m* means 'is marked for'.)

$$(3.14) \quad N \rightarrow N \quad Y^{af}_{[m\ plur]}$$

$$V \rightarrow V \quad Z^{af}_{\begin{bmatrix} m\ plur \\ m\ pers \\ m\ tns \end{bmatrix}}$$

where m = +, −, or an integer

In the formulation of these word structure rules, the affix category is specified for particular diacritic features. Given the present theory, only affixes whose lexical entries are marked for these features may be inserted into affix positions of the word structures generated by these rules. An alternative analysis of the rules would not involve this direct use of diacritic features in rules:

(3.15) N → N Y^{af}

      V → V Z^{af}

In this case, affixes could be freely inserted into these positions from the lexicon, bringing with them their own feature specifications. The inflectional system of English is too impoverished to provide a basis for judging whether word structure rules should in principle have the power to mention diacritic features, as in (3.14), or whether they could be restricted to mentioning syntactic category features, as in (3.15). When more complicated systems of inflectional morphology are examined, however, we see that it may be necessary to allow for the former possibility.

To illustrate my point, I will discuss hypothetical languages; however, since their properties are replicated throughout the world's languages, the general conclusion that I wish to draw is a valid one. As is well known, nouns are often inflected for case and/or number and/or gender. Of interest here is the fact that the features associated with these inflectional categories may be borne by a single affix, or each by a single affix, or in any other combination. That is, a language could manifest any of the following distributions of the inflectional diacritics (as well as others):

(3.16) a. $_N$[Noun   Af]$_N$

$$\begin{bmatrix} \text{m case} \\ \text{m plur} \\ \text{m gend} \end{bmatrix}$$

    b. $_N$[Noun   Af   Af]$_N$

$$\begin{bmatrix} \text{m gend} \\ \text{m plur} \end{bmatrix} \ [\text{m case}]$$

    c. $_N$[Noun   Af   Af]$_N$

$$[\text{m gend}] \ \begin{bmatrix} \text{m case} \\ \text{m plur} \end{bmatrix}$$

    d. $_N$[Noun   Af   Af   Af]$_N$

$$[\text{m gend}] \ [\text{m plur}] \ [\text{m case}]$$

(In verbs, comparable arrays of verbal inflectional diacritics for person, number, tense, aspect, mood, etc., are also possible.) A particular language will choose among these possibilities. It would seem, then, that the morphological component of a language must be able to specify the distribution of diacritic features within the word. My hypothesis is that this is done, at least in part, by the word structure rules themselves.

The word structure rules corresponding to each of the noun types in (3.16) could be written as follows:

(3.17) a. N → N   Af
$$\begin{bmatrix} \text{m case} \\ \text{m plur} \\ \text{m gend} \end{bmatrix}$$

b. N → N   Af   Af
$$\begin{bmatrix} \text{m gend} \\ \text{m plur} \end{bmatrix} \quad [\text{m case}]$$

c. N → N   Af   Af
$$[\text{m gend}] \quad \begin{bmatrix} \text{m case} \\ \text{m plur} \end{bmatrix}$$

d. N → N   Af   Af   Af
$$[\text{m gend}] \quad [\text{m plur}] \quad [\text{m case}]$$

These rules generate structures into which the affixes, listed in the lexicon as unmarked or marked for particular features, may be inserted. (The specifications $[+F_i]$, $[-F_i]$, and $[n\ F_i]$, $n \geq 1$, will be considered to be nondistinct from $[m\ F_i]$. The specification $[m\ F_i]$ is distinct from $[u\ F_i]$. Thus, an affix morpheme marked $[+\text{plur}]$ will be inserted into the $\underset{[\text{m plur}]}{\text{Af}}$ position of such a structure, while an affix morpheme that is $[u\ \text{plur}]$ may not be inserted into that position.)

The advantage of such a system of rewriting rules for inflection is that it straightforwardly captures generalizations concerning the ordering of *classes* of inflectional affixes: the class of case-marked affixes is put in relation to the class of plural-marked affixes and to the class of gender-marked affixes. If the rule system were not given the power to mention diacritic features, then the distributional relations of the affixes would have to be encoded in the subcategorization frames of the individual affixes themselves. With such an approach, a case-marked affix in a language incorporating the structure (3.16d) would presumably be subcategorized to appear to the right of the plural-marked affixes, and so on. This is the approach of Lieber (1980), for example. Under such a system, though, it is a coincidence that all case-marked affixes have the same subcategorization. Each could in principle have stipulated a different relation for itself with respect to the plural and gender affixes. The grammar would thus require some additional device for treating these affixes as a class. Rather than providing for both individual subcategorization and an additional, generalization-capturing mechanism, it seems preferable to simply adopt the theory of rewriting rules presented here, which allows a single distributional statement concerning affix classes defined in terms of diacritic features to be made for the noun, or the verb, and so on.

The expression of these generalizations regarding inflectional affix order requires that affixes be assigned diacritic features and thus that affixes belong to categories. Here, then, is one piece of evidence that affixes are not merely terminal strings, i.e., phonological entities having no categorial status of their own. This evidence supports the "mixed" theory of the morphological component over the "pure" context-free rewriting rule model.[6]

3.2.3. Percolation and the Headhood of Inflectional Affixes

Let us turn next to the question of the distribution of diacritic features within inflected structures. The structures of (3.18a) and (3.18b) illustrate a regularly inflected plural noun and a regularly inflected past tense verb in English, "before" Percolation, but "after" the mother node is marked by the syntax, and "after" (morpho-)lexical insertion:

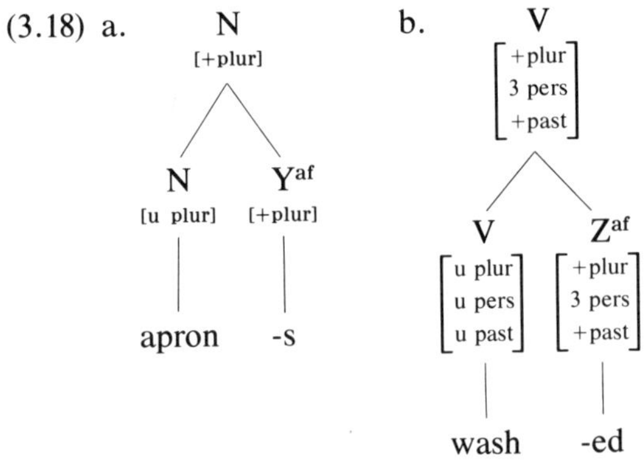

The nature of Y and Z is what we are attempting to determine. In particular, are Y and Z the heads of their respective word structures? If the answer is yes, then Y and Z will bear the features of nominal and verbal categories, respectively.

Suppose, following Williams (1981a), that the inflectional affixes are the heads of these words. This would mean that Y = [+N, −V] in (3.18a) and Z = [−N, +V] in (3.18b). The Percolation Convention (2.12) would guarantee that the mother noun or verb would bear the same diacritic features as the affix, since the latter is the head; it would thus rule (3.18a) and (3.18b) well formed. It is important to realize that, as so far defined, Percolation would ignore the relation between the mother node and the nonhead daughter constituents; hence, in (3.18a,b) it would ignore *apron* and *wash,* whose feature complexes would remain as they are. So far, this is the correct result.

When we consider languages in which words bear more than one inflectional affix whose features must be transmitted, though, the approach which defines Percolation only between a head and a mother node breaks down. I repeat the convention here:

(2.12) *Percolation*

> If a constituent α is the head of a constituent β, α and β are associated with an identical set of features (syntactic and diacritic).

We will see that once this analysis breaks down, there is little (if any) motivation for construing inflectional affixes as heads in the first place.

The problematic cases would be those involving a series of inflectional affixes, such as the word structures generated by rules of the sort mentioned in the preceding section. Consider a hypothetical (but familiar) case—a language in which one affix bears the person/number marking of the verb and another the tense marking. If Percolation is defined as in (2.12), then it is impossible to establish a lawful relation between the mother node and all of the feature-bearing affixes below it. The problem stands regardless of whether the structure of the verb in this (hypothetical) language is nested or not, that is, whether it exhibits configuration (3.19a) or (3.19b). (For the sake of argument, I assume, with Williams, that the affixes are themselves verbal, and thus (capable of being) heads in these configurations.)

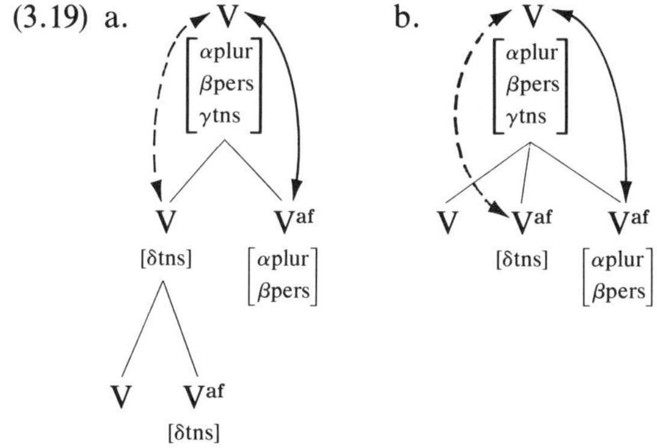

The unbroken arrows indicate "paths" of percolation, that is, nodes between which Percolation requires an identity of features, assuming a Right-hand Head Rule for this language. The broken arrows indicate nodes between which Percolation is not defined and for which the theory therefore does not require identity of features. Nevertheless, mismatches are possible. A verb marked [γtns] by the syntax would actually (wrongly) be allowed to include an affix oppositely specified for tense; in (3.19a) and (3.19b), $\delta = +$ and $\gamma = -$ is possible. These examples show that the theory of Percolation as it has been defined is too narrowly restricted, and that a more general statement is required allowing percolation relations to be established between a mother node and others of its internal constituents in addition to its head. In other words, what is required is some limited "summing up," in the mother node, of the features associated with the daughter nodes.

Specifically, I suggest the following reformulation of Percolation:

(3.20) *Percolation (revised)*

    a. If a head has a feature specification [αF$_i$], $\alpha \neq$ u, its mother node must be specified [αF$_i$], and vice versa.

    b. If a nonhead has a feature specification [βF$_j$], and the head has the feature specification [uF$_j$], then the mother node must have the feature specification [βF$_j$].

Like (2.12), (3.20) gives priority to the mother–head daughter relation, requiring the nondistinctness of their features. However, it also requires that feature specifications of other daughters be nondistinct from those of the mother node, in the event that the head daughter is unspecified for those features. Percolation as defined in (3.20) would rule out structures like (3.19a) or (3.19b) if they contained a mismatch between [γtns] and [δtns], but would correctly declare them well formed if $\gamma = \delta$.

Given (3.20), we need no longer consider inflectional affixes to be heads at all, since Percolation may be defined between the mother and its nonhead constituents as well. It is thus possible to construe the verbal base of (3.19a) or (3.19b) as the head, and to consider the syntactic features of the affixes to be unmarked, e.g., [u N, u V]. The same point could be made for the English cases (3.18a,b). If the internal noun and verb are heads, after percolation the representation of *aprons* and *washed* would be as shown in (3.18a,b), but with the mother node's feature specifications filled in on the daughter noun or verb. (Note that it is this result, the attribution of the plural features from the mother noun to the daughter (head) noun, that required that subcategorization not be construed as a well-formedness condition on (surface) representations; see the discussion in section 2.4.) While taking no strong position on the headedness of English inflected words, I will simply assume henceforth that inflectional affixes are not heads and point out that this assumption is consistent with the fact that inflectional affixes tend not to be "category-changing."

At this point, one might ask what impediment there is to saying that inflectional affixes are never heads. One nice result of this generalization would be the apparently universally attested fact that inflectional affixes are not "category-changing." If the inflectional affix is not the head, then its sister category is, and hence always shares category features with the mother node. The only difficulty is that a general condition of this sort has little force unless we have a characterization of the notion "inflectional" in the first place. Since it is not entirely clear what that characterization should be,[7] the issue is clearly moot for the time being.

3.3. English Derivational Morphology

3.3.1. The General Approach

It has long been recognized that English affixes fall into distinct classes with respect to their phonological properties. (See, for example, Newman (1946).) Chomsky and Halle take account of this in their SPE treatment of English word phonology, calling them *nonneutral* and *neutral* affixes. Siegel (1974) provides the important insight that the affix classes motivated on the basis of phonology also play a crucial role in the description of English morphology, specifically in the description of the distribution of affixes within English words. Her insight has laid the groundwork for the treatment of these affix classes that I will propose here.

My view is that this division of derivational affixes into two sets in English (Siegel's *Class I* and *Class II*) is to be explained in structural terms, that is, in terms of the place the affixes occupy in English word structure. Specifically, I will be defending the claims (i) that there are two (recursive) category levels or types that play a role in English word structure—Word, along with a "lower" category type, Root—and (ii) that Class I affixes attach to (i.e., subcategorize for) categories of type Root (and with them form roots), while Class II affixes attach to categories of type Word (and with them form words). Here, I will demonstrate that this structural analysis of the English derivational affix classes makes just the right predictions about the distribution of these affixes with respect to each other and with respect to compound structures. Elsewhere (in Selkirk (forthcoming)), I will demonstrate that this analysis provides the basis for a perspicuous and simple characterization of the relation between the word structure and the prosodic structure of English words which captures the differences in the phonological properties displayed by affixes belonging to the different classes.

Section 3.3.3 presents the category type analysis of the Class I/Class II affix distinction, as well as arguments that have been made against the Siegel/Allen approach. In section 3.3.4 I will discuss and dismiss apparent counterexamples to Siegel's Affix Ordering Generalization. In section 3.3.5 I will show that English derivational affixes of Class II do indeed "intermingle" with compounds, lending support to the category type analysis of the affix class distinction. Finally, I will argue in section 3.3.6 that the category type analysis is to be preferred to another possible theory, one based on a difference in the diacritic features naming the affixes of the two classes.

Before addressing the question of the category types involved in English derivational morphology, though, I will briefly examine the "substance" of the categories involved in English word structure, by which I mean their nominal, verbal, or adjectival properties, or, in terms of the present theory, their specification in terms of syntactic category features. This survey will give us the needed backdrop for an evaluation of competing analyses of the Class I/Class II distinction. It will also give us the opportunity to examine two other hypotheses of the $\overline{\text{X}}$ theory of W-structure: the hypothesis that all W-structures are headed (and that affixes may themselves be heads), and the hypothesis that the grammars of languages must include those particular statements that we are calling word structure rules.[8]

3.3.2. On the Headhood of Affixes and the Need for Word Structure Rules

Tables 3.1–3.3 and 3.7–3.9 provide a taxonomy of a large number (perhaps the majority) of English derivational affixes, a classification that will serve as the basis of our discussion. Tables 3.1–3.3 contain the suffixes and tables 3.7–3.9 the prefixes. The (a) sections of the tables list the types of affixed word structure configurations that I claim to exist in English, while the (b) sections give examples of affixed words which display the relevant structure. (With the exception of some pre-fixed verbs in table 3.9, I have included only examples for which the sister of the affix appears independently, and thus where its category name is clear.) Each table is organized into two subparts, labeled I and II. This organization reflects the fundamental empirical claim about English derivational morphology, which is that affixes fall into two distinct classes and that the members of one display different distributional and phonological properties from the members of the other. (A few affixes, noted with superscript "+" in the tables, may belong to either class (cf. section 3.3.4).) The assignment of some particular affixes to one class or the other (or both) has been discussed in the literature (see in particular Siegel (1974) and Allen (1978)), and some will be explicitly discussed here. However, space limitations prevent me from defending many of the assignments, all of which I have made on both morphological and phonological grounds, and for all of which I take responsibility. I leave it to the readers to assure themselves that all of the suffixes and prefixes tabulated here do indeed display the distributional and phonological properties implied by their classifications.

Let us first examine the suffixes (tables 3.1–3.3). Given the assumption that all constituents of a word are headed, it follows that an affix is the head in all cases where the category of the constituent sister to the affix is different from the category of the parent constituent. Thus, a large number of English suffixes are clearly heads, which is to say that each has the same category features as its mother. Among the suffixes which, on the other hand, are sister to X^n and with it form an X^n, e.g., $_N[_N[\text{czar}]_N$ -dom$]_N$, $_{N^r}[_{N^r}[\text{sermon}]_{N^r}$ -ette$]_{N^r}$, $_A[_A[\text{green}]_A$ -ish$]_A$, $_V[_V[\text{brok}]_V$ -en$]_V$, the situation is perhaps less clear. Consider the di-minutive suffixes -ette, -ling, -let, and so on. Semantically speaking, these are modifiers and thus would not appear to be semantically the head of the word. However, there is no evidence other than this that would rule out assigning them to the category N^{af}. Furthermore, this assignment predicts that such suffixes always make nouns in English, which in fact is the case. (See Jaeggli (1980) for a discussion of the somewhat different behavior of diminutives in Spanish.) As for the other non-"category-changing" suffixes, they are, semantically, func-tional elements of a clearly different sort from the diminutives. The suffixes -dom, -hood, -ism, for example, take as "arguments" nouns of one semantic type, making from them nouns of a different semantic type. The verbal passive -en exhibits analogous behavior. In this, all of

Table 3.1
Noun-forming Suffixes: Configurations and Examples

I. a. $_{N^r}[N^r \ N^{af}]_{N^r}$	$_{N^r}[A^r \ N^{af}]_{N^r}$	$_{N^r}[V^r \ N^{af}]_{N^r}$
b. democrac-*y*	national-*ist*	resist-*ance*
semon-*ette*	scarc-*ity*	employ-*ee*
suffrag-*ette*	Catholic-*ism*	convers-*ation*
cycl-*ist*[+]	Canadian-*a*	confus-*ion*
	decenc-*y*	orna-*ment*[+]
	wid-*th*	distill-*ate*
II. a. $_{N}[N \ N^{af}]_{N}$	$_{N}[A \ N^{af}]_{N}$	$_{N}[V \ N^{af}]_{N}$
b. sister-*hood*	kind-*ness*	sing-*er*
queen-*ship*		open-*ing*
czar-*dom*		arriv-*al*
villag-*er*		amuse-*ment*[+]
drop-*let*		slipp-*age*
squire-*ling*		
hand-*ful*		
post-*man*		
dadd-*y*		
grocer-*y*		
acre-*age*		
favorit-*ism*		
microscop-*ist*[+]		

Table 3.2
Adjective-forming Suffixes: Configurations and Examples

I. a. $_{A^r}[N^r\ A^{af}]_{A^r}$ $_{A^r}[A^r\ A^{af}]_{A^r}$ $_{A^r}[V^r\ A^{af}]_{A^r}$

     b. accident-*al*   ——   prefer-*able*[+]
         totem-*ic*   leg-*ible*
         inflation-*ary*   creat-*ive*
         adventur-*ous*   obligat-*ory*
         Canad-*ian*
         Japan-*ese*
         statu-*esque*

II. a. $_A[N\ A^{af}]_A$ $_A[A\ A^{af}]_A$ $_A[V\ A^{af}]_A$

     b. cheer-*ful*   kind-*ly*   fidget-*y*
         heart-*less*   green-*ish*   handle-*able*[+]
         friend-*ly*   blue-*y*
         pulp-*y*   near-*er*
         vultur-*ish*   near-*est*
         wood-*en*   quick-*ly* (= Adv)
         talent-*ed*
         danger-*some*

Table 3.3
Verb-forming Suffixes: Configurations and Examples

I. a. $_{V^r}[N^r\ V^{af}]_{V^r}$ $_{V^r}[A^r\ V^{af}]_{V^r}$ $_{V^r}[V^r\ V^{af}]_{V^r}$

     b. agon-*ize*[+]   prett-*ify*   ——
         cod-*ify*   activ-*ate*

II. a. $_V[N\ V^{af}]_V$ $_V[A\ V^{af}]_V$ $_V[V\ V^{af}]_V$

     b. winter-*ize*[+]   hard-*en*   mend-*ed;* brok-*en*
                                               sing-*ing*

these suffixes act quite like the "category-changing" affixes, and it is therefore plausible to consider them to be heads and to assign them the categories N^{af} and V^{af}, respectively. The suffixes *-y* and *-ish,* which make adjectives with adjectives (e.g., *greenish, bluey*), are treated here as heads, i.e., A^{af}; this is because they are the same suffixes that make adjectives with nouns (e.g., *vulturish, pulpy*), in which case they are necessarily A^{af}. On the basis of this quick survey, then, it seems possible to conclude that suffixes in English are basically the heads of their constituents, or, put another way, that they enter into configurations corresponding to the schema (3.21).

(3.21) $_{X^n}[Y^m \ X^{af}]_{X^n}$

Apparently, English is very free in the possibilities it allows for suffixation. For the most part, the types of word structure available at the level Root are the same as those at the level Word (where everything is allowed). We find two gaps in the paradigm, however: there are no instances of word structures having the configurations (3.22a) or (3.22b).

(3.22) a. $_{A^r}[A^r \ A^{af}]_{A^r}$

      b. $_{V^r}[V^r \ V^{af}]_{V^r}$

Given our approach to morphology, the grammar of English will contain a set of context-free rewriting rules for generating the word structures that *are* attested, and, as in the case of compounds, this rule system could encode the gaps. Such a rule system would be the following:

(3.23) a.
$$N^r \rightarrow \begin{Bmatrix} N^r \\ A^r \\ V^r \end{Bmatrix} N^{af} \qquad A^r \rightarrow \begin{Bmatrix} N^r \\ V^r \end{Bmatrix} A^{af} \qquad V^r \rightarrow \begin{Bmatrix} N^r \\ A^r \end{Bmatrix} V^{af}$$

b.
$$N \rightarrow \begin{Bmatrix} N \\ A \\ V \end{Bmatrix} N^{af} \qquad A \rightarrow \begin{Bmatrix} N \\ A \\ V \end{Bmatrix} A^{af} \qquad V \rightarrow \begin{Bmatrix} N \\ A \\ V \end{Bmatrix} V^{af}$$

However, it is not clear that such gaps are anything but accidental; the existence at Word level of analogues to the missing Root-level configurations (3.22a,b) would seem to suggest that the gaps do not reflect anything particularly deep about the language. A rule system for Root level which does not encode these gaps would of course be much simpler than (3.23), in the obvious sense, and could be collapsed, along with the system for Word-level rules, into the schema (3.24):

(3.24) $X^n \rightarrow Y^n \ X^{af}$

     n = Word or Root

As a point in favor of viewing this last, far simpler system as the grammar of English suffixation, consider the fact that the rule system (3.23) does little more than mirror the sum of the lexical entries for the suffixes, which are displayed in tables 3.4–3.6 corresponding with tables 3.1–3.3. These tables contain no affixes having the category A^{af} and the subcategorization [A^r ___] or the category V^{af} and the subcategorization [V^r ___]. Given a grammar that includes rule schema (3.24), the gaps are represented merely as an (accidental) fact about the lexicon (that is, the list of items it contains), not as a fact about the structural configurations possible in the language. I will assume, without further argument, that the latter is the more appropriate treatment. Note, however, that I am not maintaining that word structure rules for suffixation do not form part of the grammar of English, only that their form is quite general. As we saw in section 3.1.2, word structure rules such as the ones schematized in (3.24) are necessary in order to express language-particular generalizations concerning $\overline{X}$ levels or types, as well as the simple generalization that suffixation exists in the language.

Turning now to prefixation, displayed in tables 3.7–3.9, we will see that word structure rules of a more particular sort are required. I would like to point out first that the morphemes included in these tables form a relatively small subset of the class of morphemes that have been termed *prefixes* by grammarians such as Marchand (1969, chapter 3). The most liberal collections of prefixes include every bound morpheme of the language which may appear to the left of some other nonsuffix morpheme, and hence include elements such as those in the words *erythrocyte, bipartisan, counterproposal, microscope, monosyllable, hypersensitive*. I will argue below that some of these supposed prefixes should instead be analyzed as bound roots, and that their appearance in words is governed by rules of what has been called *nonnative compounding*. Therefore, bound morphemes such as these are absent from tables 3.7–3.9.

The morphemes of tables 3.7–3.9 share one property that is not shared by most of those that have been excluded: they each subcategorize for some specific category or categories; that is, they are not cross-categorial in their subcategorization. This is a property which in general seems to characterize affixes, as a type, and oppose them to the nonaffix categories of morphology. Admittedly, it is only a loose crite-

Table 3.4
Noun-forming Suffixes: Lexical Entries (Partial)

I.	(i) N^{af}	(i) N^{af}	(i) N^{af}
	(ii) $[N^r$ ___$]$	(ii) $[A^r$ ___$]$	(ii) $[V^r$ ___$]$
II.	(i) N^{af}	(i) N^{af}	(i) N^{af}
	(ii) $[N$ ___$]$	(ii) $[A$ ___$]$	(ii) $[V$ ___$]$

Table 3.5
Adjective-forming Suffixes: Lexical Entries (Partial)

I.	(i) A^{af}	——	(i) A^{af}
	(ii) $[N^r$ ___$]$	——	(ii) $[V^r$ ___$]$
II.	(i) A^{af}	(i) A^{af}	(i) A^{af}
	(ii) $[N$ ___$]$	(ii) $[A$ ___$]$	(ii) $[V$ ___$]$

Table 3.6
Verb-forming Suffixes: Lexical Entries (Partial)

I.	(i) V^{af}	(i) V^{af}	——
	(ii) $[N^r$ ___$]$	(ii) $[A^r$ ___$]$	——
II.	(i) V^{af}	(i) V^{af}	(i) V^{af}
	(ii) $[N$ ___$]$	(ii) $[A$ ___$]$	(ii) $[V$ ___$]$

Table 3.7
Noun-forming Prefixes: Configurations and Examples

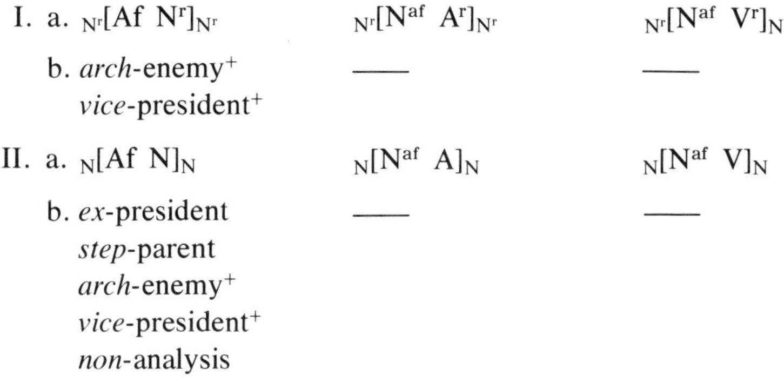

	$_{N^r}[Af\ N^r]_{N^r}$	$_{N^r}[N^{af}\ A^r]_{N^r}$	$_{N^r}[N^{af}\ V^r]_{N^r}$
I. a.			
b.	*arch*-enemy[+] *vice*-president[+]	——	——
II. a.	$_N[Af\ N]_N$	$_N[N^{af}\ A]_N$	$_N[N^{af}\ V]_N$
b.	*ex*-president *step*-parent *arch*-enemy[+] *vice*-president[+] *non*-analysis	——	——

Table 3.8
Adjective-forming Prefixes: Configurations and Examples

	$_{A^r}[A^{af}\ N^r]_{A^r}$	$_{A^r}[Af\ A^r]_{A^r}$	$_{A^r}[A^{af}\ V^r]_{A^r}$
I. a.			
b.	*a*-kin	*in*-convenient *un*-grammatical[+] *a*-new	*a*-sleep
II. a.	$_A[A^{af}\ N]_A$	$_A[Af\ A]_A$	$_A[A^{af}\ V]_A$
b.	——	*un*-convinced[+] *non*-synthetic	——

Table 3.9
Verb-forming Prefixes: Configurations and Examples

I. a. $_{V^r}[V^{af}\ N^r]_{V^r}$	$_{V^r}[V^{af}\ A^r]_{V^r}$	$_{V^r}[Af\ V^r]_{V^r}$
b. ——	——	*in*-flate
		de-flate
		ex-propriate
		con-tribute
		per-mit
		ab-solve
		de-tonate
		re-solve
		sub-stitute
		dis-pense
		inter-rupt
		trans-fer
		pre-dict
		post-pone
b'. *en*-slave	*en*-noble	*de*-centralize[+]
be-cloud	*be*-calm	*dis*-approve[+]
de-bug[+]		*be*-moan
		a-rouse
		mal-function
		un-tie[+]
		re-assemble[+]
		pre-plan[+]
		mis-represent[+]
II. a. $_{V}[V^{af}\ N]_{V}$	$_{V}[V^{af}\ A]_{V}$	$_{V}[Af\ V]_{V}$
b. *de*-bug[+]	——	*un*-tie[+]
		re-assemble[+]
		pre-plan[+]
		mis-represent[+]
		de-centralize[+]
		dis-hearten[+]

rion for prefixhood, since some morphemes of English which might seem to share this property (e.g., *erythro-*, which does not appear with verb roots) have not been included in the tables. Only a rather complete treatment of prefixation and nonnative compounding will provide a sounder basis for classifying a given item as a prefix as opposed to a (bound) root, and I will not provide that here. I would hope that the plausibility of the classification given here will be established by its ability to furnish some insight into the distributional patterns of these morphemes within English words, as well as their phonological properties.

Most prefixes of English are not "category-changing," but are rather sister to a category identical in features with the mother category, as tables 3.7–3.9 show. Given the Right-hand Head Rule, none of these prefixes will qualify as the head of its constituent, but each will have a right-hand sister as head. Thus, there is no basis for assigning them one or another array of syntactic features, a point made by Williams (1981a). It is for this reason that the category of these non-"category-changing" affixes is listed merely as Affix. The rules for generating such prefixed structures are listed in (3.25); they could be collapsed into the rule schema (3.26).

(3.25) $N^r \rightarrow Y^{af}\ N^r$ $A^r \rightarrow Y^{af}\ A^r$ $V^r \rightarrow Y^{af}\ V^r$

   $N \rightarrow Y^{af}\ N$ $A \rightarrow Y^{af}\ A$ $V \rightarrow Y^{af}\ V$

(3.26) $X^n \rightarrow Y^{af}\ X^n$

   n = Word or Root

The lexical entries for these non-"category-changing" affixes, which are listed in tables 3.10–3.12, reflect this lack of syntactic category feature assignment.

There is a small number of prefixes in English which are "category-changing"; that is, they are sister to categories whose features are not those of the mother node. These include *a-* of $_{A^r}[a\text{-}\ _{V^r}[sleep]_{V^r}]_{A^r}$ and $_{A^r}[a\text{-}\ _{N^r}[kin]_{N^r}]_{A^r}$, *en-* of $_V[en\text{-}\ _N[slave]_N]_V$ and $_V[en\text{-}\ _A[noble]_A]_V$, *be-* of $_V[be\text{-}\ _N[cloud]_N]_V$, $_V[be\text{-}\ _A[calm]_A]_V$, and *de-* of $_V[de\text{-}\ _N[bug]_N]_V$. These will be assigned the category features of their mother node, consistent with our assumption that word structures are headed and that affixes can be heads. Thus, *a-* is A^{af} and the others are V^{af} (cf. tables 3.11–3.12). Note that the Right-hand Head Rule, as revised, designates these affixes as heads: the *en-* of the verb *enslave*, for example, is the rightmost category within the structure which has the same syntactic category features as the mother category, and thus is the head. As

Table 3.10
Noun-forming Prefixes: Lexical Entries (Partial)

I. (i) Affix	——	——
(ii) [____ N^r]		
II. (i) Affix	——	——
(ii) [____ N]		

Table 3.11
Adjective-forming Prefixes: Lexical Entries (Partial)

I. ——	(i) Affix	(i) A^{af}
	(ii) [____ A^r]	(ii) [____ N^r]
II. ——	(i) Affix	——
	(ii) [____ A]	

Table 3.12
Verb-forming Prefixes: Lexical Entries (Partial)

I. (i) V^{af}	(i) V^{af}	(i) Affix
(ii) [____ N^r]	(ii) [____ A^r]	(ii) [____ V^r]
II. (i) V^{af}	——	(i) Affix
(ii) [____ N]		(ii) [____ V]

originally formulated by Williams, the RHR designated as head only the right-hand category within a word structure, so that *en-, a-,* etc., were cast as exceptions to the rule and somehow marked as heads themselves. These affixes are not exceptions to the revised version (2.11) of the RHR, though this is not to say that they are not in some sense exceptional. Under the approach outlined here, their exceptionality can be considered to lie in the fact that they appear in word structure configurations that do not conform to the general schema (3.26) for prefixed structures. Indeed, the grammar of English requires an additional set of rules for generating structures with *a-, en-,* etc.:

$$(3.27) \quad A^r \rightarrow A^{af}\ V^r \qquad V^r \rightarrow V^{af}\begin{Bmatrix} N^r \\ A^r \end{Bmatrix}$$

$$V \rightarrow V^{af}\begin{Bmatrix} N \\ A \end{Bmatrix}$$

It is the rules of (3.27) themselves which are to be qualified as marked, or exceptional, insofar as they do not conform to the general pattern defined by (3.26).

In general, one could think of the status of the more general schemata of (3.24) and (3.26) in the following way. A language will select such affixation schemata from among those universally made available by an $\overline{X}$ theory of word structure. In the unmarked case, the particular word structure rules of the language will conform to the schemata. In the marked case, however, certain rules will not. It is in this sense that the schemata form part of the grammar.

This completes our survey of the word structures and word structure rules for English affixation, viewed from the perspective of the category names (syntactic feature bundles) involved. The presentation has assumed the well-foundedness of the Word/Root category type distinction, and it is to a defense of this analysis that I now turn.

3.3.3. A Category Type Analysis of the Class I/Class II Distinction

The central empirical problem for any treatment of English derivational morphology is to correctly characterize the distinction between two classes of derivational affixes—those variously referred to as *nonneutral, Class I,* or (in the present context) *Root affixes,* on the one hand, and those referred to as *neutral, Class II,* or (here) *Word affixes,* on the other. The phonological properties which distinguish one class from the other have been the focus of most discussions of the two classes, including Newman (1946), SPE, and later works. Perhaps the most salient difference is that affixes of the second set are "ignored" or not taken into account by the principles determining the stress patterns of words (hence the term *neutral,* for *stress-neutral*), while those of the first set are not neutral in this respect but instead enter into the canonical stress patterns of English words (hence the term *nonneutral*). The second salient difference is whether or not the affixes (and segments adjacent to them within the word) are subject to certain rules of segmental phonology. This, I would claim, is to be explained largely in terms of syllabification: neutral affixes are not syllabified with their sister constituents, while nonneutral affixes are.[9] SPE explains these differences in terms of the boundary elements associated with the affixes: neutral affixes are claimed to be preceded (or followed) by the word boundary, #, and nonneutral affixes by the morpheme boundary, +, and this boundary difference is claimed to be responsible for the differential behavior of both the stress rules and the rules of segmental phonology with respect to the affixes. The Siegel/Allen theory accepts this boundary distinction and its role with respect to the rules of segmental phonology, but attributes the difference in stress properties to an extrinsic ordering of the stress rules and the rules of morphology. Both theories are untenable, given that the theory of phonological representation now gives no place to boundary elements[10] and that an extrinsic ordering of word structure rules and the principles for determining stress cannot be defined (see below).

My claim is that those differences in phonological behavior derive from, or can be explained in terms of, the place that the affixes occupy in word structure. Specifically, I suggest that in specifying the mapping between syntactic representation (S-syntactic and W-syntactic structure) and phonological representation (prosodic structure) for English, the grammar of English merely specifies that the morphological category type Root is the domain for the (cyclic) assignment of syllable structure and foot structure.[11] From this language-particular specification, taken together with various universal principles of prosodic theory, it follows that Word affixes will be stress-neutral, though Root affixes will not, and that syllable-sensitive rules of the phonology will treat the affixes in appropriately different fashion (see Selkirk (forthcoming, chapter 8)). First, however, I will argue for the morphological structure difference on which this theory of the mapping between the syntax and phonology of English words depends.

The analysis relies on Siegel's (1974) important observation that there is a pattern to the *distribution* that the non-neutral/Class I/Root and neutral/Class II/Word affixes have with respect to each other. Siegel's empirical claim, which I will call the *Affix Ordering Generalization* (AOG), is "that Class II affixes may appear outside [nonneutral] affixes, but that Class I affixes may not appear outside [neutral] affixes" (p. 163). I believe this generalization to be correct, and I will demonstrate in the following sections that it holds true for quite a variety of cases. Let us consider some examples here to get a sense of what is involved. Among the Class I affixes are, for example, the suffixes *-ous* and *-ity;* the Class II suffixes include *-less* and *-ness*. It is consistent with the AOG that the members of a single class may appear in any order with respect to each other: we find $-ous_1-ity_1$ $(monstr-os_1-ity_1)$ or $-ity_1-ous_1$ $(procliv-it_1-ous_1)$, on the one hand, and $-less_2-ness_2$ $(fear-less_2-ness_2)$ or $-ness_2-less_2$ $(tender-ness_2-less_2)$, on the other. But the order of the two classes themselves is not free. Suffixes of Class I precede those of Class II (e.g., $danger-ous_1-ness_2$, $activ-ity_1-less_2$), but not vice versa (e.g., $*fear-less_2-ity_1$, $*tender-ness_2-ous_1$). When sequences of prefixes alone are considered, no crucial evidence is to be found in favor of (or against) the AOG, for reasons to be explained below. With combinations of prefixes and suffixes, however, the AOG emerges again. Consider the Class I prefix *in-* with respect to the Class I suffixes *-ive* and *-ate,* and the Class II suffixes *-ish* and *-ness*. *In-* may appear either "inside" or "outside" the Class I suffixes, as in $[in_1-[[sensit]-ive_1]]$, $[in_1-[[sensit]-iv_1]-ity_1]$. And it appears inside Class II suffixes, but not outside of them, as in $[[in_1-hospitable]-ness_2]$ but not $*[in_1-[glutton-ish_2]]$. Or consider the Class II prefix *non-* with respect to the Class I suffixes *-ory, -al,* and *-ify* and the Class II suffixes *-er, -less, -y,* and *-ize. Non-* occurs both outside and inside Class II suffixes: $[non_2-[subscrib-er_2]]$, $[non_2-[wiggle-y_2]]$ and $[[non_2-secular]-ize_2]$, $[[non_2-nominal]-ize_2]$. (The neologisms are my own.) Prefixes also exhibit either order: $[non_2-ex_2-priest]$ and $[ex_2-non_2-believer]$. However, *non-* occurs only outside Class I suffixes: $[non_2-[preparat-ory_1]]$, $[non_2-[contract-ual_1]]$ vs. $*[[non_2-humid]-ify_1]$, $*[[non_2-electr]-ify_1]$. A theory of morphology (or a particular analysis) will be judged on its ability to capture such distributional regularities.

Siegel's (1974) hypothesis, elaborated upon by Allen (1978), is that the morphological component consists of individual rules of affixation (and compounding) which derive words from words (the more complex from the simpler) by "adding" affixes, and that these rules of word formation may be extrinsically ordered. Specifically, Siegel proposes that the rules attaching Class I affixes apply "before" rules attaching Class II affixes; in this way, she suggests, it follows that Class II will always be "outside" Class I in the linear order of morphemes. Allen elaborates this idea by proposing that the rules of the morphological component are organized into extrinsically ordered blocks or *levels,* the rules within each block being unordered with respect to each other. For English, in "order of application," the blocks are: Class I affixation, Class II affixation, inflectional affixation, and compounding. In this scheme of things, the phonological rules assigning stress are said to be ordered "after" Class I afffixation and "before" Class II affixation.

This theory faces a number of serious problems, not the least of which is that it makes incorrect predictions about the facts. As noted in section 2.4, some derivational affixes (as well as the noun plural affix) may appear outside native compounds. (3.28) provides further examples of derivational affixes with compounds.

(3.28) *Adjectives*
     a. *un*-self-sufficient, *non*-weather-related
     b. turnover-*less,* painstaking-*ly*

     Nouns
     a. *ex*-frogman, *non*-earthquake, *arch*-birdbrain
     b. laidback-*ness,* pickup-*ful*

     Verbs
     a. *re*-overthrow, *de*-upgrade, *mis*-backdate, *pre*-underline
     b. ——

More specifically, as will be shown in section 3.3.5, the generalization to be drawn from such examples is this: Class II affixes may appear inside or outside (native) compounds, while Class I affixes appear only inside (native) compounds. Let us call this the *Compound-Affix Ordering Generalization* (CAOG). These examples therefore pose grave problems for the Siegel/Allen theory, which would hold that derivational (and inflectional) affixes do not appear outside compounds. Allen (1978, chapter 4), fully aware of the significance of examples like the ones in (3.28), contends that they are either impossible or not to be generated by the rules of English morphology. However, as I will show in section 3.3.5, such a contention cannot be upheld. To meet this empirical problem in the Siegel/Allen theory, one might consider ordering Class II affixation both before and after compounding, and thereby capture the CAOG, though this move would seem to vitiate the notion of strict linear ordering of (blocks of) rules which gave rise to the AOG in that framework.

The Siegel/Allen theory encounters difficulties at the conceptual level, as well. It is not at all clear that the ordering of word formation rules and the ordering of stress rules with respect to these—both of which are essential to this hypothesis—can be defined, when one pins down just exactly what these rules of word formation are. Perhaps the most plausible model of the system envisaged by Siegel and Allen is a categorial grammar,[12] in the sense that the principle "do the innermost first" may be likened to the "bottom-up" definition of syntactic well-formedness that is basic to the categorial approach. In a categorial grammar, however, there are strictly speaking no rules, and hence no possible orderings of rules. Suppose, on the other hand, that the morphological component is not a categorial grammar, but instead, as I have argued, a context-free rewriting system. The problem facing Siegel and Allen's theory still remains: in a context-free rewriting system, there is strictly speaking no ordering of rules. However, let us suppose an "extension" of the system, one that allowed for such ordering. Within this extended system, the analogue to the Siegel/Allen ordering hypothesis would require that the rewriting rules introducing Class II affixes be ordered (in a block) *before* the rules introducing the Class I affixes. The opposite ordering would not be possible; it would give the wrong linear order of affixes, because the Class I affixes must be generated "lower" in the tree than the Class II affixes. Now, even supposing that it were theoretically possible to order stress rules among the rewriting rules of the "extended" theory (specifically, *between* the Class I and Class II blocks), the desired stressing effects could not be obtained. Class II affixation would precede the stress rules, which would precede Class I affixation. If anything, the stress rules would be analyzing Class II affixes, rather than Class I—just the opposite of what the rule ordering analysis should allow. The conclusion is that an ordering solution to the problem of the different stress-related properties of the Class I and Class II affixes is not possible within an "extended" context-free rewriting system such as this. Rather (in a theory without boundaries), the stress-related properties must be explained in terms of differences in the representation of word structure itself, in terms of the different word structure positions occupied by the affixes of the two classes. However, this version I have sketched of the Siegel/Allen ordering hypothesis offers no such characterization of the relevant differences in morphological structure, for it makes no distinctions among the categories of morphology. From this I conclude that the account proposed here is superior.

Given the theoretical framework I have outlined, distributional regularities such as the AOG and the CAOG must follow from the general properties of the morphological structure of a language and/or the idiosyncratic properties of its morphemes. A characterization of the morphological structure of a language involves an analysis of the morphological categories (defined in terms of type and feature specification) at play in the language, as well as the possible relations among these categories. This characterization takes the form of a set of word structure rules (a context-free rewriting system, with no ordering of rules) which, in conjunction with universal conventions like Percolation, define the set of well-formed morphological structures (labeled trees) for a language. As for the idiosyncratic properties of morphemes, this theory defines two sorts that are relevant to distribution: the category of the morpheme itself and the set of subcategorization frames associated with it in the lexicon.

As I have said, this theory of morphology makes available a simple and straightforward analysis of the differences between derivational affix classes in English. According to this analysis, English word structures involve two category types (besides Affix)—Word and Root; affixes are subcategorized for one or the other (or both, as we will see). The two columns in (3.29) list the subcategorization frames, as I see them, of the affixes cited in the examples discussed so far.

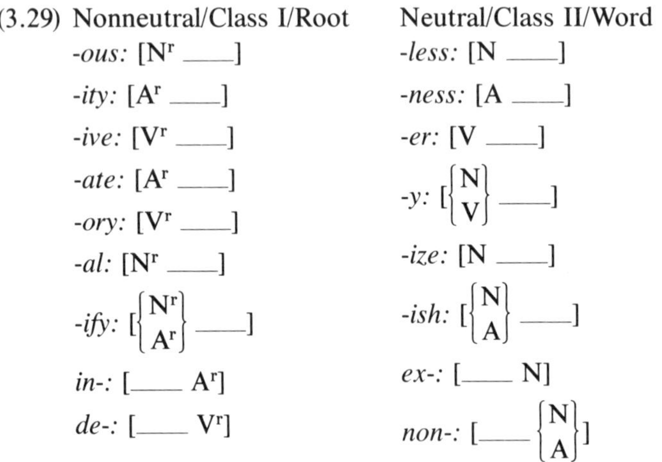

(3.29) Nonneutral/Class I/Root   Neutral/Class II/Word

Nonneutral/Class I/Root	Neutral/Class II/Word
-ous: $[N^r \underline{\quad}]$	*-less:* $[N \underline{\quad}]$
-ity: $[A^r \underline{\quad}]$	*-ness:* $[A \underline{\quad}]$
-ive: $[V^r \underline{\quad}]$	*-er:* $[V \underline{\quad}]$
-ate: $[A^r \underline{\quad}]$	*-y:* $[\left\{ {N \atop V} \right\} \underline{\quad}]$
-ory: $[V^r \underline{\quad}]$	
-al: $[N^r \underline{\quad}]$	*-ize:* $[N \underline{\quad}]$
-ify: $[\left\{ {N^r \atop A^r} \right\} \underline{\quad}]$	*-ish:* $[\left\{ {N \atop A} \right\} \underline{\quad}]$
in-: $[\underline{\quad} A^r]$	*ex-:* $[\underline{\quad} N]$
de-: $[\underline{\quad} V^r]$	*non-:* $[\underline{\quad} \left\{ {N \atop A} \right\}]$

Clearly, in any theory, an affix must be allowed to subcategorize for (choose, select, or whatever) the category *name* (features) of its sister. I am proposing merely that morphological categories may have different *type* specifications and that an affix may select for one (or more) of these, in addition to choosing a set of category features. These subcategorizations will guarantee the proper distribution of affixes in English words, given the rule systems (3.24) and (3.26)/(3.27).

Recall that (3.24) and (3.26) are themselves a schematization of the schemata (3.30a) and (3.31a), which, ignoring the variables for category features, could be informally written as (3.30b) and (3.31b).

(3.30) a. $X \rightarrow Y^{af}\ X$ b. Word $\rightarrow$ Affix Word
          $X \rightarrow Y\ X^{af}$ Word $\rightarrow$ Word Affix

(3.31) a. $X^r \rightarrow Y^{af}\ X^r$ b. Root $\rightarrow$ Affix Root
          $X^r \rightarrow Y^r\ X^{af}$ Root $\rightarrow$ Root Affix

The rules of (3.30) and (3.31) thus define two discrete subsystems of English derivational morphology, one involving Word and one involving the lower category Root. Given the general hypothesis (1.9) concerning the relations between category types within words, a Root (complex or simple) will always be lower than, or contained within, the Word in word structure. Necessarily, the grammar includes a rule (schema) which in effect "connects" the levels. I believe that it must have the form (3.32), which collapses the rules in (3.33).

(3.32) a. $X \rightarrow X^r$ b. Word $\rightarrow$ Root

(3.33) $N \rightarrow N^r$
          $A \rightarrow A^r$
          $V \rightarrow V^r$

(Alternatively, one could imagine that there were instead, or in addition, rules of the form Word $\rightarrow$ Root Affix and Word $\rightarrow$ Affix Root, but there seems to be no need to posit such rules in characterizing possible word structures of English.) It seems, then, that (3.24), (3.26), and (3.32) form the complete system of rule schemata for English derivational morphology. Together they generate an (infinite) array of structures, into which the items listed in the lexicon may be inserted.

Table 3.13 includes a representative sampling of the word structures generated, specified only with respect to category type, along with a list of words displaying each type of structure. (Some of the examples have further structure at the Root level that is not illustrated.) It should be

Table 3.13
Structures of English Affixed Words

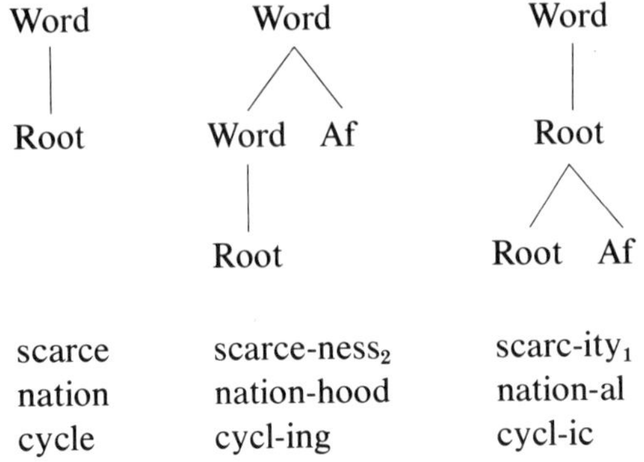

scarce   scarce-ness₂   scarc-ity₁
nation   nation-hood   nation-al
cycle   cycl-ing   cycl-ic

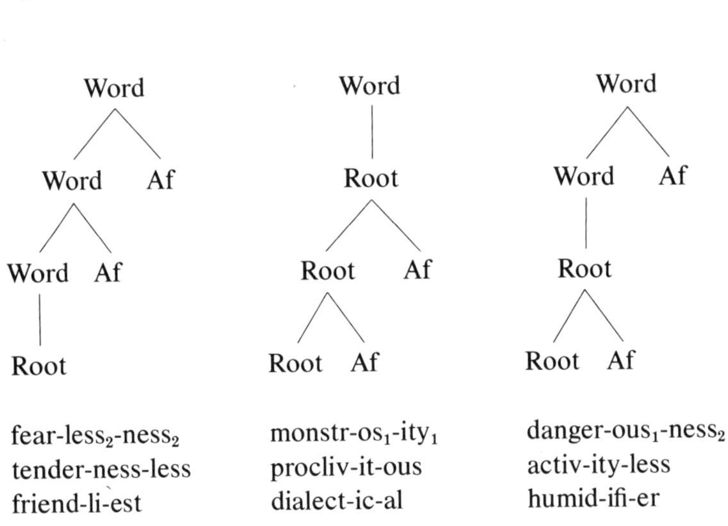

fear-less₂-ness₂   monstr-os₁-ity₁   danger-ous₁-ness₂
tender-ness-less   procliv-it-ous   activ-ity-less
friend-li-est   dialect-ic-al   humid-ifi-er

Table 3.13 (continued)

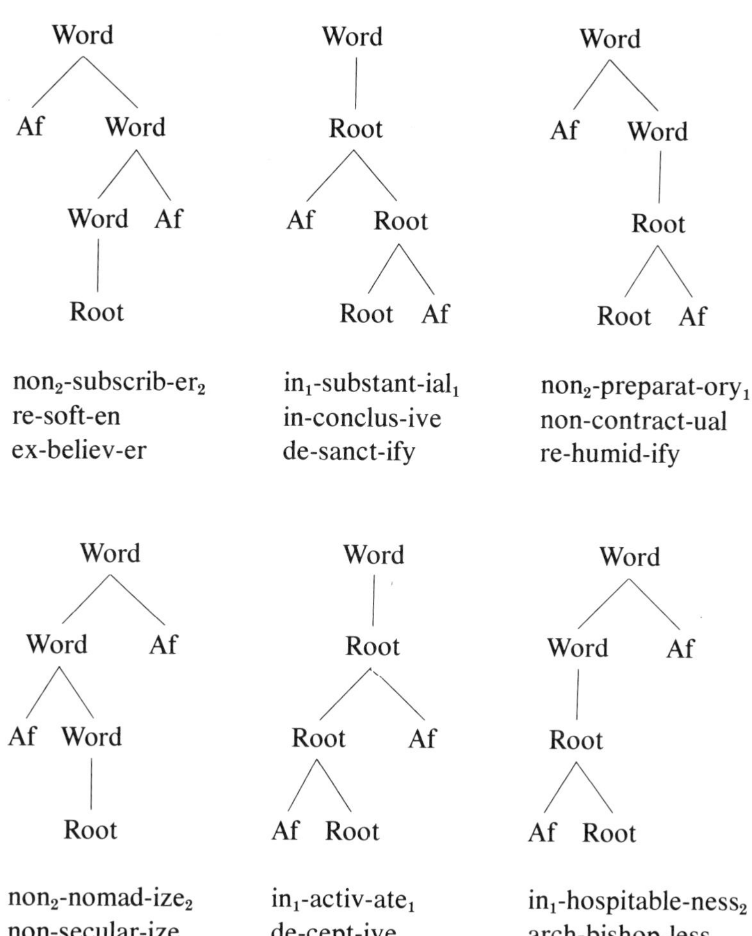

non$_2$-subscrib-er$_2$
re-soft-en
ex-believ-er

in$_1$-substant-ial$_1$
in-conclus-ive
de-sanct-ify

non$_2$-preparat-ory$_1$
non-contract-ual
re-humid-ify

non$_2$-nomad-ize$_2$
non-secular-ize
un-kind-ness

in$_1$-activ-ate$_1$
de-cept-ive
en-noble-ment

in$_1$-hospitable-ness$_2$
arch-bishop-less
de-ceiv-er

clear from the examples and the rule schemata that all of the grammatical orderings of Class I and Class II affixes are generated, but none of the ungrammatical ones. A Root (Class I) affix will never appear "outside" a Word (Class II) affix, for the simple reason that the former will always be generated "below" the latter, given the structures proposed here.

In an earlier, unpublished version of this monograph and in Selkirk (1978, 1980a), I proposed that (ignoring affixes) English word structure displays a three-way category type distinction among Root, Stem, and Word. The Root/Stem distinction was proposed to capture the Class I/Class II affix distribution, while a Stem/Word distinction was thought to be necessary for a description of inflectional morphology and compounding. As I pointed out in section 2.4, however, not only is there no basis for a Stem/Word distinction in the grammar of compounding and inflection; such a distinction makes incorrect predictions about the facts as well. We are therefore left with a single level—Word—relevant to inflection and (native) compounding. This is also the category involved in the structure of words with Class II affixes. It will become increasingly clear as the discussion develops that the two-way type distinction, Root vs. Word, is adequate for describing the full range of English word structures. The term *Root* is chosen here for the category type lower than Word partly in order to reserve for the term *Stem* its more or less traditional association with a level relevant to inflectional morphology.

In this system, the status of an item as a *root* does not imply that it is bound (that is, not free to appear alone in a word and hence in a sentence, unassociated with a sister in some word structure). Here every monomorphemic nonaffix morpheme is redundantly a root, and in principle it may also be a word. The system assigns the adjective *sad* the structure $_A[_{A^r}[sad]_{A^r}]_A$. A certain number of roots do exist that are bound, however, such as the italicized parts of *moll*-ify, de-*ceive*, *erythro*-cyte. Call them *bound roots*. It is not entirely clear to me how the restriction on the free distribution of these morphemes should be imposed in the grammar. One possibility, of course, would be to assign the bound roots a subcategorization, like affixes. This is a plausible proposal, given that bound roots tend to demand something either on their right or on their left. The verb root *-ceive*, for example, requires a prefix; it could be given the subcategorization frame [Affix ____]. The adjective root *moll-* demands a suffix, and so could be listed with the frame

[____ Affix]. The bound root *erythro-* could be subcategorized for a root on its right, [____ Root]. Such an approach presupposes that the notion of subcategorization in morphology is in principle considerably more liberal than it has been in syntax, where only elements which may be the heads of phrases would appear to have subcategorization frames. *Mollify,* for instance, exhibits a "category-changing" suffix which is the head and which subcategorizes for an adjective (or noun) root, as well as a bound adjective root which, on this theory, would subcategorize for an affix. The freer approach to subcategorization sketched here is further rendered plausible by already existing evidence that elements which are not heads of their constituents in word structure do have privileges of distribution which must on this theory be represented by subcategorization frames: prefixes are not heads, for the most part, but they all subcategorize for a particular category to appear on their right. If this approach is correct, it would seem that in morphology the notion of subcategorization is strictly syntactic and cannot be conflated with the semantic properties of the item that is subcategorized.

In the discussion thus far, the category type Root has played a role only with respect to affixation, but there is reason to believe that compounding (specifically, nonnative compounding) is also defined at this level. The facts about nonnative compounds are consistent with a treatment of them as compound roots. I would (tentatively) propose, therefore, that Root is a recursive compounding category as well, and that the morphological component of English contains rules of the form (3.34).

(3.34) Root → Root Root

Examples like the ones in (3.35) are quite plausibly analyzed either as Root–Root compounds or as structures containing Root–Root compounds, the latter being defined by (3.34) and the rules Root → Affix Root and Root → Root Affix.

(3.35) mono-syllable	nulli-par-ous	auto-mobile
bi-partite	micro-scope	tri-sect
erythro-cyte	franco-phile	photo-synthesis
ethno-centr-ic	anti-path-y	intra-mur-al
multi-ply	counter-fact-ual	ultra-reaction-ary
meta-theoret-ical	poly-gon	extra-curricul-ar

Earlier analyses in the generative framework regarded the left-hand elements of many of these examples as prefixes (cf. SPE (p. 34), Siegel

(1974)). Here I am suggesting that they and the morphemes on their right are roots. Unfortunately, space does not permit a thorough defense of this analysis. I offer it merely as a suggestion, one which arises naturally within the analysis of English word structure being proposed here and which, on the face of it, seems entirely consistent with the distribution of these morphemes.

3.3.4. Dual Membership in Class I and Class II

As noted by Siegel (1974, 105), Aronoff (1974, 1976), and others, while the vast majority of English affixes belong either to Class I or Class II (that is, they are either Root affixes or Word affixes), some belong to both. The fact that an affix may be a member of both classes can easily be expressed in the context of the present theory: in the subcategorization frame of the affix, the type of the category for which it subcategorizes may simply be left unspecified for Root vs. Word, as in [____ X^n] or [X^n ____], n = Word or Root. In the following discussion, I would like to examine certain affixes that have this dual status and compare them with affixes belonging only to one or the other class.

Consider first the adjective prefixes *in-*, *un-*, and *non-*, all of which are negative in force. (Cf. Allen's (1978) discussion of these prefixes.[13]) As I have already illustrated, *in-* is strictly a Class I affix and hence does not appear "outside" Class II affixes, while *non-* is strictly a Class II affix, appearing only "outside" Class I. However, *un-* must apparently be assigned to both classes. Such differences are represented in the three prefixes' subcategorization frames:

(3.36) *in-:* [____ A^r]

     non-: [____ A]

     un-: [____ A^n]   (n = Word, Root)

Un- has all of the properties of a Class II (Word) affix. It may appear outside (native) compounds, as (3.28) shows, and it occurs outside other Class II affixes: [un-[health-y]], [un-[daunt-ed]], [un-[fear-ful]], [un-[ghoul-ish]], [un-[cling-y]]. However, it also appears inside a Class I affix such as *-ity*. The adjectives of (3.38) must all be given the analysis (3.37a), not (3.37b), since *un-* appears only with (is only subcategorized for) adjectives, not nouns.

(3.37)

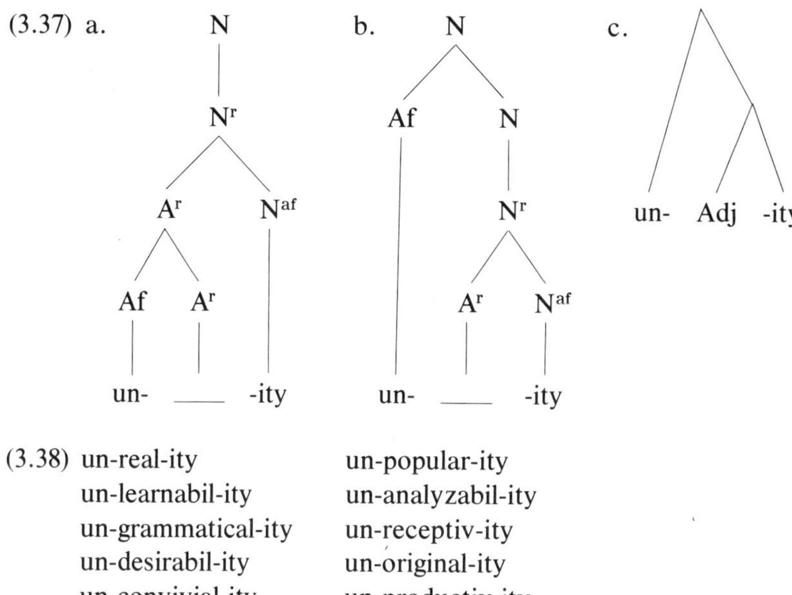

(3.38) un-real-ity   un-popular-ity
        un-learnabil-ity   un-analyzabil-ity
        un-grammatical-ity   un-receptiv-ity
        un-desirabil-ity   un-original-ity
        un-convivial-ity   un-productiv-ity

Williams (1981a) argues that the constituency (3.37c), roughly that of (3.37b), is possible for the examples of (3.38) and therefore that *un-* can retain its status as a Class II affix only. Williams claims that this constituency is possible because the semantic interpretation of words cannot in general be said to be compositional and must in general allow nonsisters in word structure, such as *un-* plus Adj in (3.37c) or (3.37b), to be interpreted as a semantic unit. But while Williams's general point is well taken (see the following section for further discussion), it is not relevant to the cases at hand. Even with a noncompositional semantics, this theory would not admit such a structure as (3.37c) (or (3.37b)) given that *un-* is subcategorized for adjectives and not for nouns.[14] This basic fact about *un-* has been taken up in many works (cf. especially Siegel (1973)), and I will not repeat the discussion here. Suffice it to say that, given this subcategorization, *un-* cannot be inserted into a structure such as (3.37c) (or (3.37b)). The conclusion, then, is that *un-* belongs to two classes, both I and II.

Treating *un-* as a member of both morphological classes predicts that it will display the phonological behavior of either. That is, with respect to stress (especially foot structure) and syllabification, *un-* could behave like *in-*, on the one hand, and like *non-*, on the other. In fact, it turns out that the stress system of English provides no means of distinguishing between Class I and Class II prefixes. Selkirk (forthcoming) demonstrates that neither the basic principles assigning prosodic structure (in particular, foot structure) nor the rule of Initial Defooting (i.e., Initial Destressing) allows one to say that *un-* must be a Word affix as opposed to a Root affix in any particular instance. The same work argues (contra Allen (1978)) that the occasional stress differences exhibited by the three negative prefixes *in-, un-,* and *non-* cannot be explained in terms of their class membership. There is one additional phonological factor which has been taken to indicate that *un-* (and *non-*) can (never) be in the same class as *in-*. The prefix *in-* is realized with a final coronal nasal only before vowels and homorganic obstruents: *inactive, intolerant, insubstantial.* Before an obstruent, the nasal consonant assimilates in place: *impractical, incongruous* [ɪŋk...]. Before a sonorant, it disappears altogether: *illegal* [ɪlij...], *irreverent* [ɪr...], *immaterial* [ɪm...]. *Un-*, however, behaves quite differently. The *n* remains before sonorants and only sporadically assimilates before a nonhomorganic obstruent: *unnoble* [ʌnno...], *unmildewed* [ʌnm...], *unreceptive/unreceptivity* [ʌnri...], *unlearnable/unlearnability* [ʌnl...], *unproductive* [ʌnp... ~ ʌmp...], etc. It can be argued, though, that the phonological alternations exhibited by *in-* are not dependent on the prosodic structure of the utterance, and therefore that they do not reveal that *in-* occupies a different place in morphological structure from *un-* or *non-*. Rather, the alternations are appropriately characterized by rules of allomorphy which are sensitive to morphological structure and, more specifically, to the diacritic features associated with the (labeled bracketing of) the morphemes: *in-* can quite reasonably be assigned a diacritic feature that is not borne by *un-* or *non-*. In sum, I am claiming that there is no phonological evidence which prevents us from viewing *un-* both as a member of the same affix class as *in-* and as a member of the same class as *non-*.

Other prefixes besides *un-* occupy a variable position in word structure, as do a few suffixes. Among the noun prefixes, *arch-* and *vice-* belong to both classes, while *ex-, step-,* and *non-* belong only to Class II:

(3.39) *arch-:*   [arch-[offend-er$_2$]]   [[arch-imperialist]-ic$_1$]
       [arch-[war criminal]]   [[arch-heretic]-al$_1$]

   vice-:   [vice-[overseer$_2$]]   [[vice-president]-ial$_1$]
       [vice-[chairperson]]   [[vice-minister]-ial$_1$]

ex-:	[ex-[[believ]-er$_2$]]	*[[ex-patriot]-ic$_1$]
	[ex-[frog-man]]	*[[ex-president]-ial$_1$]
non-:	[non-[scrubwoman]]	*[[non-exempl]-ify$_1$]
	[non-[offend-er$_2$]]	*[[non-nomad]-ify$_1$]

Among the verb prefixes, a fair number are restricted to Class I; some
of these are the ones with which bound verb roots may appear (see
table 3.9). These include *ab-, con-, sub-, trans-, in-,* etc., and *dis-, mal-,
en-, be-*. There are also some verb prefixes that belong to either Class I
or Class II (e.g., *re-, mis-, pre-, un-, de-*), but apparently none that is
restricted to Class II. The distributional privileges of various of these
prefixes are illustrated in (3.40):

(3.40) *re-:*	[re-[undercut]]	[[re-defin]-ition$_1$]
	[re-[overthrow]]	[[re-populat]-ion$_1$]
mis-:	[mis-[backdate]]	[[mis-represent]-ation$_1$]
	[mis-[underline]]	[[mis-educat]-ion$_1$]
pre-:	[pre-[upgrade]]	[[pre-insert]-ion$_1$]
	[pre-[outflank]]	[[pre-exist]-ence$_1$]
de-:	[de-[upgrade]]	[[de-populat]-ion$_1$]
	[de-[backdate]]	[[de-stabiliz]-ation$_1$]
dis-:	*[dis-[forestall]]	[[dis-associat]-ion$_1$]
	*[dis-[undermine]]	[[dis-infect]-ant$_1$]
mal-:	*[mal-[upgrade]]	[[mal-adapt]-ation$_1$]
	*[mal-[underline]]	[[mal-assimilat]-ion$_1$]

The last two, *dis-* and *mal-,* are only two of a considerable list of prefixes limited to Class I.

We are now in a position to understand why the Affix Ordering Generalization (AOG) cannot be illustrated with prefix sequences. It is due
to the simple fact, presumably accidental, that the noun and verb prefixes contain no sets that are strictly disjoint: both types include affixes
belonging to both Classes I and II, and, beyond that, only affixes of one
particular class. Noun prefixes are either Class I/II or II, and hence
noun prefixes which are Class I (also II) may appear outside the strictly
Class II prefixes; verb prefixes are either Class I/II or I, and hence
those that are Class II (also I) may appear inside the strictly Class I
affixes. Only the adjective prefixes are disjoint in their classifications:
in- is strictly Class I, and *non-* is strictly Class II. But here no examples
with both can be constructed, for the irrelevant (and independently

motivated) reason that sequences of two negative affixal elements are not allowed. (See Siegel (1977), Allen (1978).) The interaction of prefixes with suffixes, however, makes it quite clear that they too fall under the AOG, as demonstrated above.

Finally, let us examine the few instances of suffixes that belong to both Class I and Class II. There are two suffixes *-ment* (Aronoff (1974, 54) and Siegel (1977)), two *-able* (Aronoff (1974; 1976, 120ff.)), and two *-ize* (SPE, 153–154). These suffixes are of particular interest, because it is with just these that Aronoff (1976, 84–85) constructs what he deems to be counterexamples to the AOG. Consider first the examples *governmental* and *developmental*. As Aronoff points out, *-al* is a nonneutral (Class I) affix; in these words, he argues, it appears outside neutral (Class II) *-ment* and hence constitutes a counterexample to the AOG. However, Aronoff argues that there are two suffixes *-ment* in English—one affixed to bound roots like *ornament* and one to verbs like *employment*. Aronoff points out that the suffix *-al* freely attaches to *-ment* forms of the first sort (*ornamental*) but never (except with *government* and *development*) to *-ment* forms of the latter sort (**employmental*). Siegel (1977) draws the conclusion, with which I concur, that the former *-ment* is a nonneutral (Class I) affix and the latter a neutral (Class II) affix. What then of *government, development*, which both allow *-al?* These are exceptions, in that no other Verb + *-ment* form takes *-al*. My suggestion is that *government* and *development* have been reanalyzed (in effect, recategorized). Formerly words of the shape $_N[_V[_{V^r}[...]_{V^r}]_V$ -ment$]_N$, these two have now been reanalyzed as roots which have the shape $_{N^r}[_{V^r}[govern]_{V^r}$ -ment$]_{N^r}$. As such, they may receive the affix *-al*. Certainly the existence of the Root affix *-ment* in examples like *ornament* must have facilitated such a reanalysis: now *government* and *development* behave just like *ornament* and the other Root forms. I am arguing, then, that *governmental* and *developmental* are not true counterexamples to the AOG, but instead involve instances of a (sporadic) reanalysis of words as roots, one made possible by an analogy with the roots *ornament, excrement,* etc., which have an identical suffix.

A similar sort of explanation can be given for another set of apparent counterexamples to the AOG, adduced by Aronoff (1976, 84–85). As Aronoff points out (pp. 121ff.), there are two suffixes *-able* in English, a Class I type that has an allomorph in *-ible* (e.g., *indefensible, incontestable*) and a Class II type that occurs in such words as *reroutable*[15] (whose analysis I take to be $_A[_V[re-\ _V[_N[route]_N]_V]_V$ -able$]_A$). The problem for the AOG is that the Class II affix *-ity* appears to be able to follow both types: *incontestability* and *reroutability*. Other examples with seemingly neutral *-able* include *analyzability, challengeability,* etc. One could argue, however, that every instance of the *-ity* suffix following *-able* involves reanalysis of the *-able* form as a derived root, on the model of the existing derived roots containing the nonneutral *-able:* $_N[_{N^r}[_{A^r}[_{V^r}[\text{analyze}]_{V^r}\text{-able}]_{A^r}\text{-ity}]_{N^r}]_N$.

The remaining apparent counterexample to the AOG cited by Aronoff is the word *standardization. -Ation* is a Class I (nonneutral) suffix, and the claim is that it appears in this word outside an instance of the Class II (neutral) *-ize.*[16] As with the other cases, however, it could be argued that *standardize* is reanalyzed as a root (on analogy to the root *-ize* forms such as *catholicize, amortize,* etc.).

For all of these apparent counterexamples to the AOG, I have suggested that a reanalysis of words as roots has permitted the affixation of nonneutral affixes "outside of" what appear to be neutral affixes. I have suggested that such a reanalysis is made possible by the independent existence of homophonous nonneutral affixes in the language, thereby predicting that no such reanalysis would be possible were no such analogy available. But what about the stress patterns of words like *developmental, analyzability,* and *standardization?* Here the roots *develop, analyze,* and *standardize* retain (in the relevant aspects) the stress pattern they would have if they preceded neutral affixes. Aronoff claims that this is not the pattern they would have if the inside affix were nonneutral (Class I). How can our analysis account for this, given the reanalysis of *development, analyzable,* and *standardize* as derived roots? The answer, I believe, is that words are listed with their stress patterns in the lexicon (see, for example, Selkirk (1980a)). When reanalyzed as roots, they retain that same stress pattern and thus continue to display it when subsequently combined with affixes such as *-al* and *-ity.* This notion that stress is represented in lexical entries, though by no means standard, is not a new one (cf. Siegel (1974), Aronoff (1976), Roeper and Siegel (1978), Selkirk (1980a)).

To sum up: in this section I hope to have contributed to establishing the well-foundedness of Siegel's Affix Ordering Generalization by providing an explanation for the apparent counterexamples to it. The apparent counterexamples involve affixes which may appear inside and outside both Class I and Class II affixes. My claim is that such affixes themselves belong to both Class I and Class II. The reason that this solution does not call the AOG itself into question is that there exist (a substantial number of) other affixes that belong only to one or the other. It is with this latter sort that the AOG emerges.

In the following section, one of my purposes will be to establish the well-foundedness of the Compound-Affix Ordering Generalization (CAOG). The analysis of English compounds and derivational affixes that I have offered predicts that Word affixes (Class II) should be able to attach to (appear "outside of") compound words (the native compounds), and that Root affixes (Class I) should not be able to do so. As we will see, this prediction is borne out.

3.3.5. The Intermingling of Compounds and Affixes

Given that the rules of compounding are of the general form Word → Word Word and that the grammar contains affixation rules of the form Word → Word Affix and Word → Affix Word, it is predicted that affixes may appear outside compounds. (The rewriting rules involving affixation at the level Word cannot in principle "know" whether the Word generated as sister to Affix will be rewritten as a compound or not.) However, it is also predicted that only affixes which are themselves subcategorized for sisters of type Word (i.e., Class II affixes) will be able to appear in such configurations.

Example (3.28) gave lists of Class II affixes attaching to compounds. These lists are expanded here, with attention first to prefixes:

(3.41)

Adjectives	*Nouns*	*Verbs*
a. un-self-sufficient	c. ex-football coach	f. re-undercut
un-easygoing	ex-frogman	re-overthrow
un-homesick	ex-cleaning woman	re-outflank
un-heartfelt	ex-fallout shelter	g. de-backdate
un-bloodthirsty	ex-Redcoat	de-upgrade
un-outmoded	ex-prom queen	de-underline
un-downtrodden	d. non-earthquake	h. mis-backdate
un-light-sensitive	non-hardback	mis-underline
un-top-heavy	non-meter feeding	mis-upgrade
un-germ-resistant	e. arch-birdbrain	i. pre-undersell
un-outstanding	arch-dimwit	pre-outflank
un-uptight	arch-war criminal	pre-underline
un-laidback		

b. non-light-sensitive
   non-weather-related
   non-trance-inducing
   non-nationwide
   non-skintight
   non-overripe
   non-bluegreen
   non-redhot

Compare these examples to the ungrammatical combinations that result when a (strictly) Class I prefix attaches to a native compound:

(3.42)

Adjectives	*Nouns*	*Verbs*
a. *in-self-sufficient	b. (There are no	c. *dis-backdate
*in-self-evident	strictly Class I	*dis-upgrade
*in-light-sensitive	nominal prefixes.)	*dis-underline
*in-outmoded		d. *mal-upgrade
*in-germ-resistant		*mal-undersell
		*mal-outflank

This array of facts gives support to the analysis of English word structure that I have been proposing.

Under this analysis, structures of the types (3.43a–c) may be assigned to the examples of (3.41):

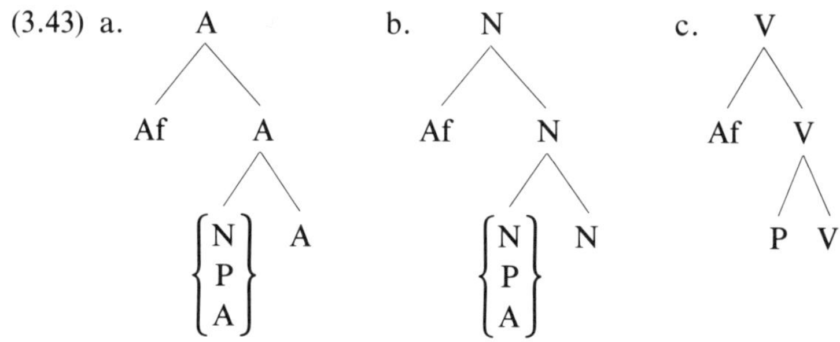

An alternative analysis is possible for some words, according to which the affix is attached to the first member of the compound and therefore lies *within* it:

(3.44) a.

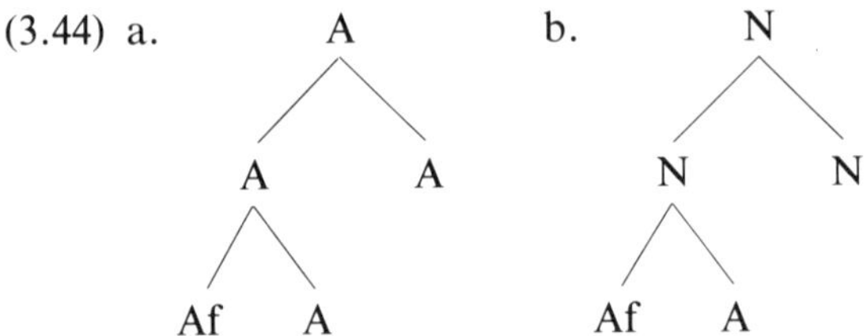

This would in principle be possible for *archbirdbrain, ex–prom queen, unlaidback,* and *nonnationwide,* given Williams's notion of the non-compositionality of semantic interpretation within words. However, this alternative does not exist for most of the examples given in (3.41), and they must be assigned one of the structures in (3.43). The prefixed compound verbs involving *re-, mis-, pre-, de-* can be assigned no other analysis than (3.43), for the prefixes involved subcategorize for Verb, not Preposition, and prepositions are the first internal category within these compounds. Among the prefixed compound adjectives, looking merely at those with *un-,* it is clear that *un-* must be analyzed as a prefix to the compound as a whole whenever the first element of the compound is a noun or a preposition and therefore does not meet *un-*'s subcategorization. Where the nominal prefixes are concerned, examples such as *ex-Redcoat* are crucial, for *ex-* is subcategorized for Noun and thus cannot be prefix to *red* within the compound.

Any examples which must necessarily be assigned the structures in (3.43) are problematic for the Siegel/Allen theory, which makes the explicit claim that no affixes appear outside of compounds (given that, on their theory, all affixing "precedes" all compounding). In fact, Allen explicitly denies that combinations of *un-* plus adjective compound are well formed. However, this claim is false, as the grammaticality of the examples in (3.41) shows. To be sure, there are examples with this structure which are ill formed, such as **uncolorblind, *unhomemade, *undownfilled, *unberrygathering, *unhandwashable,* which Allen cites (1978, 222). (Compare also **unblind, *ungathering.*) However, it is fair to say that the ill-formedness of these examples is semantic: it seems that *un-* may felicitously attach only to adjectives that have a degree interpretation (ones that could be modified by quantifiers such as *more, so, very,* and so on), for instance, *unthoughtful, very thoughtful* vs. **ungovernmental, *very governmental.* The compound adjectives with *un-* display this same pattern: *untopheavy* (cf. also *so untopheavy, very topheavy* vs. **unnationwide, *very nationwide*). I conclude that the compound adjectives prefixed with *un-* are indisputably well formed.

Presuming the well-formedness of the examples in (3.41), it is still possible that the morphemes being called prefixes here are not prefixes, but Words, and that the examples have the structure of compounds throughout, e.g., Word[Word[un-] Word[Word[top] Word[heavy]]]. Under this analysis, such words would not be counterexamples to Siegel and Allen's rule-ordering hypothesis. For this alternative to be consistent, suffixes would also have to be analyzed as Words, for prefixed compounds appear inside suffixes ([[un-self-conscious]-ness], [[un-heart-felt]-ness], [[ex-politician]-less], [[ex-priest]-ish]), as do compounds without prefixes ([[laid-back]-ness], [[sit-in]-less]). However, treating prefixes and suffixes as Words is unacceptable; we will see in section 3.4 that affixes belong to a category type Affix that is distinct from Word.

A fair number of Class II suffixes, in particular *-ness* and *-less,* appear to follow compounds quite readily. One encounters forms as complex as *humpbacked whaleishness* and as simple as *stuckupness.* Among these, though, there are only a few types which actually demonstrate that suffixes indeed attach to compounds: those in which the suffix attaches to a noun or adjective compound whose right-hand member is a preposition (particle):

(3.45) *Nouns*

stuck-up-ness	runaway-hood	a pickup-ful of kids
laid-back-ness	standby-hood	a dugout-ful of soldiers
grown-up-ness	goof-off-hood	
worn-out-ness		

Adjectives

a handout-less existence	a cutoff-ish look to it
a kickback-less record	a put-on-ish flavor to it
a turnover-less administration	a sellout-ish way of behaving
a send-off-less departure	a standoff-ish remark
a sit-in-less strike	
a standby-less flight	

In such cases, the suffixes, subcategorized either for nouns or adjectives, cannot be seen as attaching to an internal member of the compound (in this case a preposition) and so must be analyzed as sisters to the compound as a whole:

(3.46) a.

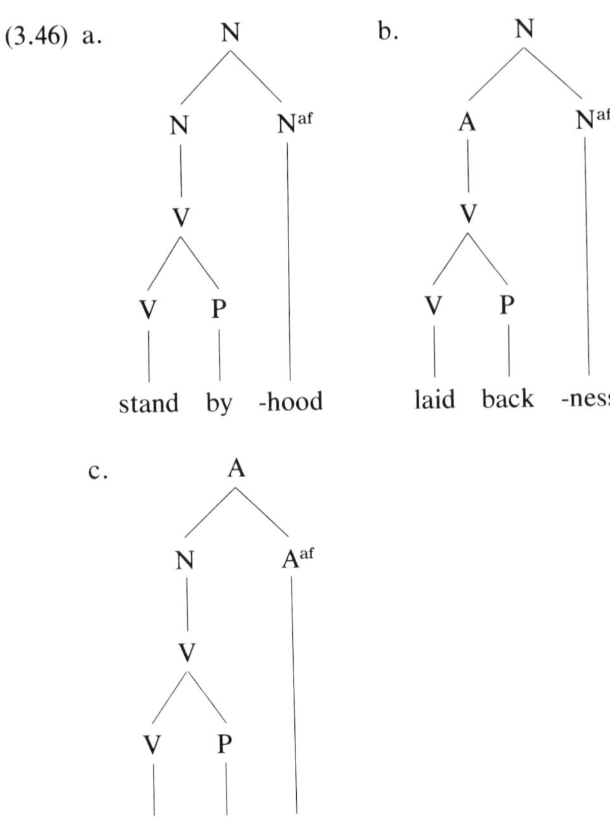

It is important to note that Class I suffixes are impossible with such compounds, as predicted.

(3.47) *laid-back-ity
      *standby-ic
      *turnover-al

Next consider suffixes that appear with (normal) right-headed compounds. In such cases, the category of the right-hand member is the same as the category of the compound itself. The analysis presented here therefore predicts a systematic structural ambiguity for Class II suffixes appearing with such compounds, assigning either the structures of (3.48b) or those of (3.48c):

(3.48) a. bathroom-less   headstrong-ness   carpetbagg-er
           pighead-ed   maidservant-hood   painstaking-ly

   b. $_A[_N[_N[bath]_N \; _N[room]_N]_N$ -less$]_A$
      $_N[_A[_N[head]_N \; _A[strong]_A]_A$ -ness$]_N$

   c. $_A[_N[bath]_N \; _A[_N[room]_N$ -less$]_A]_A$
      $_N[_N[head]_N \; _N[_A[strong]_A$ -ness$]_N]_N$

   d. ((bathroom) -less)
      ((headstrong) -ness)

The suffix *-less,* for example, has the subcategorization frame [N ____],
which is satisfied in the structures of both (3.48b), where *-less* is sister
to the compound noun as a whole, and (3.48c), where *-less* is internal to
the compound but again sister to a noun. In either case, the structure
can be assigned the proper semantic interpretation. The structures of
(3.48b) can be interpreted in normal compositional fashion; the structures of (3.48c) can be interpreted as well, and given the same interpretation as those of (3.48b), following the principle allowing for
noncompositionality in the interpretation of word structure suggested
by Williams (1981a). This principle has the effect of allowing structures
like those of (3.48c) to be interpreted according to the bracketing
shown in (3.48d). It should be apparent, then, that examples of right-
headed compounds followed by Class II suffixes do not provide crucial
evidence for the CAOG or the claim that the structures of (3.48b) are
possible (though they are consistent with it), since such examples may
also have the analysis (3.48c). (See Levi (1978) for discussion of combinations of this sort.)

Examples like those of (3.49a), where Class I affixes follow and appear to attach to right-headed native compounds, are not a problem for
the analysis I have proposed.

(3.49) a. set theoretic
           noun phrase cyclic
           South American

   b. $_A[_N[set]_N \; _A[theoret-ic]_A]_A$
      $_A[_N[noun \; phrase]_N \; _A[cycl-ic]_A]_A$
      $_A[_A[South]_A \; _A[Americ-an]_A]_A$

The grammar given will assign the examples of (3.49a) only the structures of (3.48b), for Class I affixes are all subcategorized for Root cate-

gories and thus cannot appear "outside" native compounds like *set theory, South American,* and *noun phrase cycle.* As Williams points out, a structural analysis such as (3.49b) is entirely acceptable for these forms, for it will be assigned the proper interpretation, given the non-compositionality of semantic interpretation in word structure. The words of (3.49) are therefore quite consistent with my claim that Class I affixes attach only to roots.

I have shown here, with examples like *unselfconscious, reunderline, laidbackness,* and *turnoverless,* that the grammar generates Class II affixes outside of native compounds. This is as predicted, since Class II affixes are Word affixes, and native compounds are words. I have also shown that there are no crucial cases demonstrating that Class I affixes appear outside native compounds. This is predicted as well, in that Class I affixes have been analyzed as Root affixes. What we see, then, is an intermingling of compound structures and affixed structures (with Class II affixes)—a state of affairs that is predicted, given the analysis that the category types involved in both sorts of word structure (and hence in the rules for generating them) are the same.

3.3.6. Against a Diacritic Analysis of the Class I/Class II Distinction

In this section I will consider an alternative description of the Class I/Class II affix distribution which does not rely on positing the category type distinction Word vs. Root, but instead explains the distinction on the basis of the system of features assigned to the various affixes and the other categories. This sort of alternative can be readily formulated within the theoretical framework developed here, and it may indeed be appropriate for other languages. As we will see, however, it has significant drawbacks with respect to the English morphological system, and hence is not a viable alternative in this case to the proposed category type analysis.

Under the feature-based theory, all word structure rules in English would belong to the schemata Word $\rightarrow$ Word Affix, Word $\rightarrow$ Affix Word, and Word $\rightarrow$ Word Word. The affixes of the two classes would have to differ in two ways: first, they would be differently (oppositely) specified for some arbitrarily chosen diacritic feature, say [$\pm$L]; and, second, they would demand different specifications for this particular feature in their subcategorization frames. A seemingly viable analysis of this sort is summed up in (3.50):

(3.50) *Category*   *Subcategorization Frame*
                                      Prefix   or *Suffix*

Class I {Af; α, +L, ...}   [___ β] or [β ___]
                                          $_{[+L]}$ $_{[+L]}$

Class II {Af; α, −L, ...}   [___ β] or [β ___]
                                          $_{[\pm L]}$ $_{[\pm L]}$

(where α, β stand for a specification in terms of the syntactic category features [±Noun], [±Verb])

I will call this the *diacritic analysis*. Together with the universal convention on Percolation and the notion of the headedness of word structures, the diacritic analysis appears at first blush to be able to capture the basic facts concerning the distributional possibilities of affixes from the two classes (the AOG). Class I affixes are assigned the feature [+L] (i.e., belong to the category [+L]). Thus, if a Class I affix is the head of its constituent, that higher constituent will also be [+L], by Percolation. This analysis also specifies that Class I affixes subcategorize for sister constituents that are [+L]; that is, they may attach to constituents which themselves have a [+L] affix as head. However, they will not attach to constituents containing a head which is a Class II affix; the latter are [−L], with the result that the constituents of which they are head are also [−L] and thus would not satisfy the Class I subcategorization frame. (Note that for the Class I affixes to be able to attach to nonaffixed, monomorphemic entities, it must be the case that the grammar specifies all of these, redundantly, as [+L].) As for the Class II affixes, on this analysis they are specified [−L] (and hence would not, if heads, appear inside a [+L] affix), but they are given subcategorization frames which permit them to adjoin to either [+L] or [−L] constituents; therefore, they may attach to monomorphemic bases, or to bases containing either a Class I or Class II affix as head.

There is one further point to be made here. This analysis presupposes either that subcategorization frames are well-formedness conditions on full representations to which Percolation has already "applied," or that lexical insertion and Percolation are cyclic. One of these two alternatives is necessary, since the subcategorization frames of the affixes mention features of a sister constituent which that sister might bear only as a "result of" Percolation. In discussing related issues in section 2.4, I concluded that the first option was not viable. Consequently, I will assume here that the second must be adopted. The (cyclic) insertion of an affix on a lower cycle and cyclic Percolation will ensure that, if the affix is the head, the diacritic features of the affix are associated with its mother node. On the next higher cycle, those features will be available to scrutiny by the lexical insertion transformation, which will (as in the standard view) allow for the insertion of an affix on that (higher) cycle only if the subcategorization frame of the affix, defined partly in terms of those features, is met.

Let us examine words involving sequences of suffixes, such as those with the structures in (3.51). The words of (3.51a–c) are well formed, but (3.51d) is not:

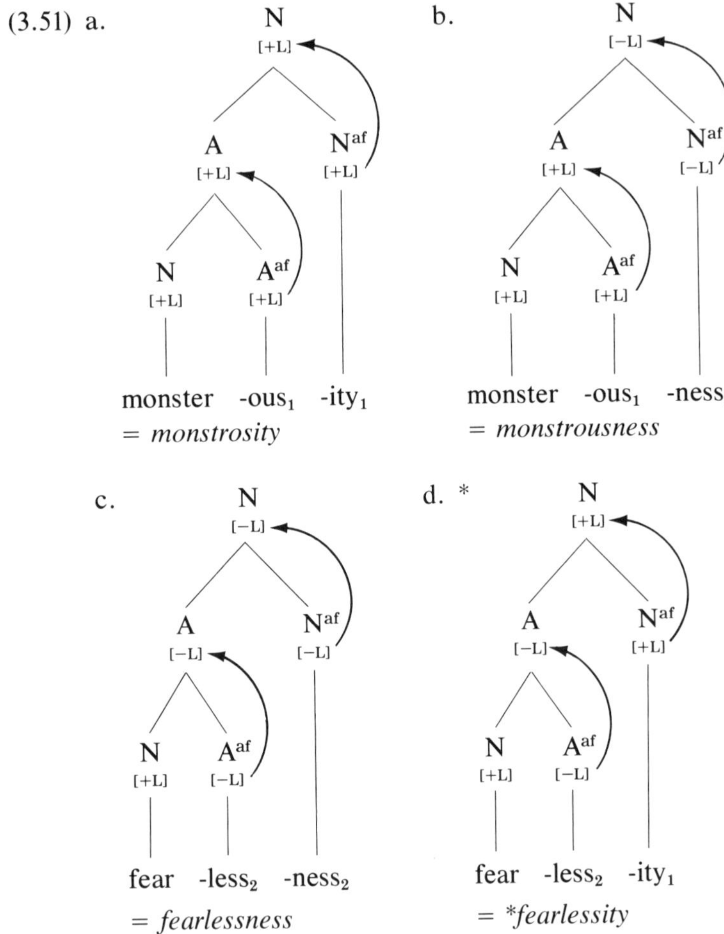

(The curved arrows indicate the paths of Percolation.) As a Class II suffix, *-ness* has a subcategorization frame allowing it either a [+L] or a [−L] sister: [A ___]. Its subcategorization frame is thus met in either
$$[\pm L]$$
(3.51b) or (3.51c). Moreover, since the subcategorizations of the suffixes on the lower cycle are met as well, (3.51b) and (3.51c) are well formed. As a Class I affix, *-ity* has a subcategorization frame calling only for a [+L] sister: [A ___]. That frame is met in (3.51a), but not
$$[+L]$$
in (3.51d), where the lower [−L] affix gives the potential sister of *-ity* a [−L] designation. Thus, (3.51d) is not a possible word, in contrast to (3.51a), where the subcategorization frames of the affixes are met on all cycles. Thus far, then, it would seem that the diacritic analysis permits a characterization of the Affix Ordering Generalization.

The diacritic analysis is also able to account for suffixes that are members of both Class I and Class II. Consider *-able,* which on the earlier analysis was subcategorized for a Verb sister of any level; that is, it had the subcategorization frame [V^n ___]. Under the diacritic analysis, on the other hand, the freedom of *-able* to appear inside and outside an affix of any class could be expressed if *-able* were not specified for the diacritic, but were instead itself [u L], and if this *-able* were subcategorized for sisters of either specification, that is, had the frame [V ___]. Given this subcategorization, *-able* could appear in
$$[\pm L]$$
either of the configurations in (3.52).

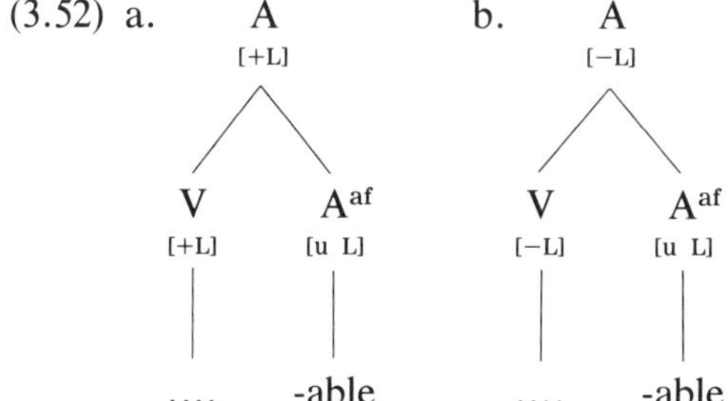

Moreover, because *-able* is [u L], it will not lend its feature specification for [L] to the mother node, which will instead receive the feature specification of the sister of *-able,* following the revised version of Percolation, (3.20). Thus, *-able* is in a sense invisible with respect to further affixation, the nature of its mother with respect to [±L] being determined by its (nonhead) sister. As a result, Class I *-ity* may attach if the sister is [+L]. A Class II suffix could attach to either of the two configurations with *-able*.

Thus far, the diacritic analysis does seem to be a viable alternative to the category type analysis. However, both empirical and theoretical shortcomings emerge when we consider the diacritic analysis from a somewhat broader perspective. Notice first that although the diacritic analysis is observationally adequate, it is deficient from the point of view of descriptive adequacy. The diacritic analysis of the affix classes relies on the specification of two independently variable properties of an affix: its own category (either [+L] or [−L], among other things) and its subcategorization frame (specified for the [+L] and/or [−L] quality of the sister). Such an approach predicts the possible existence of affixes displaying all combinations of these two independently varying properties. In addition to the affix classes of (3.50), one might expect to encounter those of (3.53).

(3.53) *Category*   *Subcategorization Frame*

[−L] $[\ \beta \underline{\quad\quad}\ ]$ or $[\underline{\quad\quad}\ \beta\ ]$
              $\quad {}_{[+L]}$ $\qquad\qquad {}_{[+L]}$

[+L] $[\ \beta \underline{\quad\quad}\ ]$ or $[\underline{\quad\quad}\ \beta\ ]$
              $\quad {}_{[-L]}$ $\qquad\qquad {}_{[-L]}$

[−L] $[\ \beta \underline{\quad\quad}\ ]$ or $[\underline{\quad\quad}\ \beta\ ]$
              $\quad {}_{[-L]}$ $\qquad\qquad {}_{[-L]}$

[+L] $[\ \beta \underline{\quad\quad}\ ]$ or $[\underline{\quad\quad}\ \beta\ ]$
              $\quad {}_{[\pm L]}$ $\qquad\qquad {}_{[\pm L]}$

[u L] $[\ \beta \underline{\quad\quad}\ ]$ or $[\underline{\quad\quad}\ \beta\ ]$
              $\quad {}_{[-L]}$ $\qquad\qquad {}_{[-L]}$

    etc.

The fact that none of these classes exists in English does not seem to follow from any properties of the theory as a whole. Given the diacritic analysis, it is an accident that there should exist only a subset of the available possibilities, and that it should be the particular subset of (3.50). It is (3.50) that gives rise to the Affix Ordering Generalization effects. By contrast, the category type analysis allows only for the attested possibilities. Given the category type distinction Word vs. Root, the possibilities are strictly limited: an affix may subcategorize for one or the other type, or both. One tenet of the general theory of types or levels in morphology is that one type will dominate another, and not vice versa, which means that an affix subcategorized for one type will always appear "outside" an affix subcategorized for the other. The category type analysis explains why there should exist only affixes of the two classes (and affixes of either); it is thus descriptively adequate and superior to the diacritic analysis.

The diacritic analysis has two other shortcomings, of which I will first mention the more obvious. By eliminating category type distinctions, the diacritic analysis would treat the category type of compounds as identical to the category type of monomorphemic or affixed words. As a result, though, it is unable to explain why Class I affixes cannot appear "outside" compounds; that is, it cannot give a characterization of the Compound-Affix Ordering Generalization. In particular, if a compound had a [+L] head constituent and were thus [+L] itself (by Percolation), the diacritic analysis would wrongly predict that the compound would be capable of taking a Class I prefix or suffix. The ungrammatical form *inlightsensitive*, (3.54), would thus be predicted to be well formed, since the subcategorization restriction of the Class I prefix *in-*, which would be [____ A], would be met.
[+L]

(3.54)

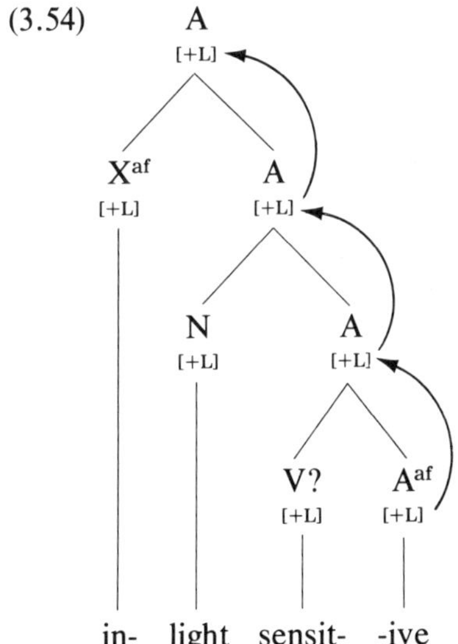

To avoid this result, it would not be possible to stipulate that Percolation of diacritics does not extend "up" into compounds, because a theory that makes no appeal to category types has no straightforward way of identifying a compound level as opposed to a noncompound level. Even if such levels could be identified, it would be incorrect to prohibit percolation between them, for a proper treatment of plurals relies on such "interlevel" percolation (cf. section 2.4). Thus, the diacritic analysis is at an impasse, making the wrong predictions about the facts in one way or the other.

As a final point against the diacritic analysis, we will see that it cannot provide an observationally adequate account of the distributional properties of prefixes with respect to other affixes. The problem is this. Given the general theory of percolation, the features of nonheads will not be in a percolation relation to the features of the mother node if the feature specifications of the nonheads are distinct from those of the head. This means that the [±L] specification of nonhead prefixes will not percolate to the mother, and therefore that no nonhead prefix will determine what sorts of affixes (Class I or Class II) may be sister to the mother node. In the case of a constituent containing a nonhead prefix, it is the [±L] specification of the head word that percolates. But consider now the prediction made with respect to the Class II prefix *non-*. *Non-* is not a "category-changing" prefix; it is therefore not the head of its word. Like all Class II prefixes, *non-* may attach to constituents containing either Class I or Class II suffix heads; its subcategorization frame is [____ ±L]. If this is the case, though, we would expect that when *non-* attaches to a [+L] word, the mother node dominating *non-* and its sister head is [+L], by Percolation, and we would thus predict that a Class I affix should be able to be sister to that mother node. This, of course, would violate the AOG, and it does not seem to be permitted; witness such an example as **nonhumidify*. To avoid the problem, the diacritic analysis would require a change in the theory of percolation, according to which any affix, whether head or not, would have priority in "percolating" its features to the mother node. This modification in the theory would have consequences that I will not explore here, given that the drawbacks of the diacritic analysis are otherwise considerable enough that this attempt at salvage is pointless.

In sum, I have demonstrated that, of two different devices made available within the general theoretical framework for describing the affix classes in English morphology, an analysis relying on a distinction in category types is superior to one based on diacritic features. At this point, I am hesitant about drawing sweeping conclusions on the basis of this demonstration. That is, I am not persuaded that an analysis making comparable use of diacritic features should be excluded in principle. It does not seem correct that the theory should allow only for an appeal to category types in the subcategorization frames of affixes, for example. Nonetheless, it seems clear that, for English, it is the category type analysis that correctly characterizes the distributional possibilities available to affixes.

3.4. Affix as Category

The context-free grammar for word structure that I have been defending assumes a theory of morphological categories specified in terms of types (or levels) and features (or names). This theory of categories makes it possible to express the distributional properties of affixes, for example, without recourse to statements about the (extrinsic) ordering of affixation rules. In other words, it allows the model of word formation to retain the character of a true context-free grammar, in which an ordering of rules is not defined.

I have shown for English that positing the nonaffix category types Word and Root allows the distribution of the two classes of derivational affixes (and the distribution of the inflectional affixes) to be characterized in a perspicuous and straightforward way, capturing just the appropriate generalizations. This is of course what is required of a theory—that it allow for descriptively adequate treatments of linguistic phenomena. In addition, a theory must restrict the class of possible grammars. The theory of word structure proposed here has just that restrictive character—it holds that word structure is generated by a context-free grammar, a model whose properties are well understood and which defines an extremely limited class of languages.

Two models of a grammar of words have in fact been entertained. According to one, a "pure" context-free grammar, the set of rewriting rules generates terminal strings (as well as strings of nonterminal vocabulary). In particular, each affix morpheme (terminal string) is introduced by a separate rule of the system, of the form A → B *abc* (where A, B are nonterminal, and *abc* is a terminal string), for example. In this way, each rule introducing an affix morpheme encodes the distributional possibilities of that particular affix. According to the other, a "mixed" model, the context-free rewriting rules generate strings of nonterminal symbols (typically represented as a labeled tree or bracketing), but do not introduce the material of the terminal string. Affix morphemes, like nonaffix morphemes, are assigned to a category. Morphemes, or complex morphological structures, are introduced into the word structures generated by the rules via the sort of lexical insertion described in *Aspects*. On this theory, the distributional peculiarities of affixes, like those of other entities, are represented as following from (a) their category membership and (b) their subcategorizational requirements.[17] The critical difference between the two models is the assignment of affix morphemes to categories. With the "pure" context-free grammar, affixes do not have a categorial status; in the "mixed" model, they do. In this section I will argue for the "mixed" model, on the grounds that it allows for a descriptively adequate characterization of word structure and of word-structure-dependent phenomena, and that such a characterization is not possible within a "pure" context-free grammar. I will argue, in particular, that affixes must be assigned to categories and moreover that there exists a special category type *Affix* that is distinct from the category types Word, Root, Stem, etc.

Note first, though, that the distribution of the English Class I and Class II affixes—either with respect to each other or with respect to compounds—can be characterized properly within a "pure" context-free grammar. Thus, it is not these particular distributional facts that push us on to the "mixed" theory. A distinction between two category levels in the system of rewriting rules is enough to guarantee this distribution. Below is a fragment of a "pure" context-free grammar of English word structure:

(3.55) a. $N \rightarrow non\ N$ b. $X \rightarrow X^r$ c. $A^r \rightarrow un\ A^r$
          $A \rightarrow non\ A$ $A^r \rightarrow in\ A^r$
          $A \rightarrow un\ A$ $\vdots$
          $\vdots$

For each of the Class II affixes, there is a rule rewriting a Word-level category as that affix morpheme plus another Word-level category. For each of the Class I affixes, there is a rule rewriting a Root-level category as Affix plus Root-level category. In addition, there is a general rule (3.55b), which makes for the transition between the Word and the Root levels. Like the account given in section 3.3.3, which was couched in a "mixed" theory, this analysis would permit the AOG and the CAOG to be explained in terms of the place in word structure occupied by the affixes of the two classes—Class II affixes are still viewed as sister to Word and Class I as sister to Root.

It must be acknowledged, though, that a grammar like (3.55) fails to capture certain other types of generalizations. First, and perhaps foremost, such a grammar cannot express the fact that English prefixes are (with a few exceptions) not "category-changing," while the suffixes are. The theoretical principle of "one rule per affix" denies that such generalizations are significant, and thus would seem to fly in the face of the facts. Second, the necessity of stating a separate rule for every configuration in which an affix may appear in effect denies that the "same" affix appears in two (or more) configurations. (3.55) gives two rules introducing *non-*, $N \rightarrow non\ N$ and $A \rightarrow non\ A$, and two rules for introducing *un-*, $A \rightarrow un\ A$ and $A^r \rightarrow un\ A^r$. It is thereby cast as coincidental that the two cases of *un-* and *non-* share more than a homophonous terminal string. Surely this misses a generalization.

Consider again how the mixed theory permits a grammar which does capture these generalizations. The first sort of generalization, regarding the general form of possible affixed structure in English, is encoded by the rule system of (3.56), which is a set of schemata for rules rewriting the particular categories, specified in terms of features (names) as well as type:

(3.56) a. $X \rightarrow Y^{af}\ X$ b. $X \rightarrow X^r$ c. $X^r \rightarrow Y^{af}\ X^r$
       $X \rightarrow Y\ X^{af}$ $X^r \rightarrow Y^r\ X^{af}$

Example (3.56) is not a fragment; it comprises the full set of rules responsible for defining well-formed (abstract) affix structures in English (aside from the small number of rules for exceptional cases, given in (3.27)). It expresses the generalization that prefixes are not "category-changing," while suffixes are. The rule system of (3.56) (and a rule system for compounds), together with the lexicon, defines the possible affixed words of English.

Consider next the lexical entries of (3.57), which comprise a fragment of the full lexicon of English.

(3.57) *non-:* a. Y^{af} *in-:* a. Y^{af} *un-:* a. Y^{af}

       b. $[\underline{\quad} \begin{Bmatrix} A \\ N \end{Bmatrix}]$ b. $[\underline{\quad} A^r]$ b. $[\underline{\quad} A^n]$
                                                                 $n = $ Word,
                                                                 Root

       c. SR_{354} c. SR_{197} c. SR_{76}

       d. [nan]   d. [ɪn]   d. [ʌn]

The single affix *non-*, with its phonological representation [nan] and its semantic representation SR_{354}, has a double subcategorization, which allows it to appear as sister to Noun or Adjective. *Un-*, whose meaning is defined by SR_{76} and whose phonological representation is [ʌn], also has a dual subcategorization, for an adjective of either the Word or the

Root type. It is in the lexicon, then, that the sameness of an affix appearing in two different configurations may be expressed. We see, then, that the richer, more fully articulated "mixed" theory—with its two components, the context-free rewriting rules and the lexicon—permits the expression of linguistically significant generalizations which the simple, "pure" context-free rewriting system does not.

The possibility of expressing generalizations about word structure in rules like (3.56) and the possibility of representing the sameness of affixes in the lexicon as shown in (3.57) require that affixes be identified with a category. The generalizations captured in (3.56) concern categories, not individual morphemes. The identity of two instances of an affix is captured in a shared lexical entry, and it is the assignment of a category to that lexical item that contributes to ensuring the proper distribution by lexical insertion of that morpheme in the word structures, which are defined by the rules in terms of that category and others.

An additional argument for the categorial status of affixes was made in section 3.2, and concerned the distribution of inflectional affixes. I argued that it was necessary to be able to formulate word structure rules in terms of categories specified with (diacritic) inflectional feature bundles in order to be able to state generalizations regarding the distribution of classes of affixes defined in terms of such notions as case, plurality, etc. It of course follows from this that the affix morphemes themselves must be characterized in terms of such features, which is to say that they must be assigned to categories specified in terms of such features.[18]

A final point to be made concerns the category type Affix. The discussion of the grammar (3.56)/(3.57) assumed not only that affix morphemes are assigned to a category, but also that that category is of the special type Affix. An alternative (within the confines of a theory of categories as a pair (type, name)) would be to consider that affixes belong to some other category of the morphology, say Word, Root (or Stem). On this theory, affixed structures would simply be special cases of compounds, affix morphemes perhaps being distinguished from non-affix morphemes merely by the fact of being bound, i.e., having an obligatory subcategorization.[19] Consider an example. An affix which forms an adjective with a noun has the syntactic features $[+N, +V]$. If it were of type Word, then it would be an Adjective, which is to say that *stony,* on this theory, would have the structure $_A[_N[\text{stone}]_N \ _A[\text{-y}]_A]_N$ and would thus be structurally the same as *stone deaf,* $_A[_N[\text{stone}]_N$

$_A$[deaf]$_A$]$_N$. The second prediction made by this theory is that the word structure rules required for generating affixed words would be the same as those generating compound words.

Both of these predictions are false. That compound word structure is *not* identical to affixed word structure emerges when we consider rules of the grammar which apply to, or interpret, morphological structures. This is most notable in the case of rules governing (ultimately) the phonetic realization of words—be they morphophonemic rules or rules of the syntax–phonology mapping (including the prosodic well-formedness conditions). An affix is simply not treated like a word by such processes. Ample evidence of this is available in any treatment of English stress, for example (among them SPE and Selkirk (forthcoming)). Suffice it to say here that such rules must "know" whether a morpheme is an affix or not. Compound words do not have the same phonology as affixed words.

The second prediction is also unsupported, as a look at the word structure rules for English compounds and derivational morphology will show. The system of derivational morphology would require the rules in (3.58) to replace those in (3.59), given the assumption that affixes are of the type Word.

(3.58) a. V → N V   (3.59) a. V → N V^{af} (e.g., *winter-ize*)
      b. V → A V   b. V → A V^{af} (e.g., *soft-en*)
      c. A → V A   c. A → V A^{af} (e.g., *fidget-y*)

However, it has already been pointed out that (real) compounds of the sort that (3.58) would generate are not found in English. (See the discussion of this matter in section 2.1.)

Because the theory that affixes are of the same category type as nonaffix elements makes these wrong predictions, I will assume instead that a difference between the two is to be represented in morphological structure. In particular, I propose that Affix be assigned a type of its own, X^{af}. With this type specification, the word structure rules introducing affixes and compound structure are distinct statements, not to be conflated, and the structures that they generate encode just the differences that are relevant for the operation of interpretive processes of the grammar.

The type Affix has two properties that distinguish it from the categories Word and Root that have been posited for English (and from the Stem, or further such levels, that might play a role in the grammar of other languages). First, the category Affix seems to be necessarily preterminal. Recursive embeddings of Affix within Affix have not been attested; moreover, Affix apparently dominates neither Word nor Root. The second property distinguishing Affix from Root or Word is that it is always sister to a nonaffix category type in word structure. For these reasons, it seems appropriate to view the category type Affix as falling "outside" the $\overline{X}$ hierarchy within which Word is of level zero (i.e., X), the next lower category (e.g., Root in English) is X^{-1}, and so on. To capture these facts in a notational fashion, I will simply assign the category type Affix a constant, $a,$ instead of an integer. This constant will be interpreted as being less than zero (and Affix thereby a category "lower than" Word), but it will enter into no further general $\overline{X}$ relations with categories of the other types.

Notes

Chapter 1

1. See Lapointe (1980a,b) and Lieber (1980) on the inclusion of inflection in the morphological component of a grammar.

2. There seem to be syntactic processes which create words having an internal structure, specifically words consisting of words. This is commonly thought to be the case with the syntactic cliticization of pronouns and other elements. For example, on most accounts, the surface syntactic structure of nonsubject pronoun plus verb combinations in French, such as *les mangez* '(you) eat them', is $_V[_{Pro}[les]_{Pro} \ _V[mangez]_V]_V$. Kayne (1975) and others argue that this structure is derived by syntactic transformation. Rivas (1977), Morin (1978), Grimshaw (1982), and others argue that this structure is generated by the phrase structure rules of the base. Supposing that either one of these analyses is correct and that such structures cannot be said to be generated by rules of word structure, i.e., of the morphological component (as suggested by Lapointe (1980a)), then these are instances where it must be said that rules of the syntactic component participate in the "construction" of words. But this sort of case does not contradict the general model being proposed: it is to be expected that the rules of syntax will manipulate units of the category level Word, as in cliticization, for words are units of the syntax as well as of the morphology.

3. See Lapointe (1980a), who develops a theory of morphology and syntax which presupposes the autonomy of the two systems.

4. Roger Higgins suggested the terms *W-syntax* and *S-syntax* to me.

5. It has come to my attention that in his dissertation Jindrich Toman (1978–79) elaborates a theory of word syntax which is similar in many respects to the one described here. I am unfortunately not able to take account of his work here, but will leave a comparison of the two approaches and an evaluation of their relative merits for the future.

6. Allen (1978) explicitly dismisses a context-free rewriting system as a model for the generative component of morphology (see pp. 8–9). The grounds given for this dismissal are shaky, to say the least. Allen admits that the word struc-

tures of English could indeed be generated by a system of rules such as (i), for example.

(i) A → N, *ed*   A → N, *al*
    A → N, *less*   A → N, *ous*
    A → V, *ive*   A → V, *ory*
    A → N, *ic*

But she asserts that the sheer number of these rules shows that this is the wrong way of looking at things, that morphology cannot be like syntax. In Allen's words, having so many rules for rewriting a category is a ". . . situation [that] is not found in syntax; it is practically inconceivable to have, say, ten ways of rewriting S, or twelve ways of rewriting VP" (1978, 9). Of course, it is not inconceivable that there should be many ways of rewriting VP, for example. This is precisely the situation that would obtain if there were no preterminal category Verb, for example. It is entirely conceivable that it might occur to someone to invent a model of syntax which had such rules. Of course, not many would be willing to advocate such a model, since it so blatantly misses generalizations. This does not mean that the baby should be thrown out with the bathwater, though. With a sufficient enrichment in terms of categories, a context-free rewriting system is eminently capable of capturing basic generalizations about the phrase structure of language. The same point can be made for morphology. Merely by assigning affixes a categorial status, it is possible to avoid stating the plethora of rules in (i) and to capture real generalizations about word structure with a much streamlined rewriting system. Such an approach is outlined immediately below in the text.

7. Whether or not all phrases are headed is of course a matter for debate among syntacticians. In particular, some assume that the Sentence is not headed, while others hold that the Sentence is a verbal category whose head is VP. See Jackendoff (1977) for some discussion.

8. My earlier position was that Word, Stem, and Root were all required for a description of English morphology. I now believe that only two category levels are involved in English. See sections 2.4 and 3.3 for discussion.

9. In fact, Jackendoff employs a feature system that differs from Chomsky's, but the difference is irrelevant to the point at hand. Whether there is a decomposition of syntactic category names into feature complexes in the first place is also irrelevant. Nor does it matter whether or not the specifications "+" and "−" are required. For the sake of discussion, I adopt the position of Chomsky (1970) on the status of syntactic and diacritic features.

10. On the basis of a study of verbal compounding in Afrikaans, Botha (1980) challenges the assertion that syntactic phrases do not enter into "word formation." However, as his work has reached me too late to be evaluated here, the debate will have to be left for a later time.

   Mohanan (1982) argues that two levels of compounding exist in Malayalam and that either type can appear within the other. Here also, I have not been able to assess the merits of the case, and so leave its resolution for future research.

11. In a recent dissertation, Stowell (1981) argues that the rules generating S-structure in language are not "particular" in this way. Specifically, he argues that phrase structure rules do not mention category names, only category types. His position is that the other seemingly particular aspects of phrase structure follow from general principles of grammar, such as those involved in the theory of case. Though I have not yet been able to examine the dissertation, my argument below concerning the necessity of language-specific rules for particular W-structure configurations is at odds with the general line that Stowell takes.

12. But see Toman (1978–79), who shares my concern with word syntax. See also Lapointe (1980a,b).

13. I assume, with Lapointe (1980a,b) and Lieber (1980), that both derivational and inflectional morphology are "lexical," in the sense that the rules of the morphological component, and not the syntactic component, define the well-formedness of both derived and inflected items. It does not follow from this, however, that all derived or inflected items are lexical items (that is, elements of the list being called *the dictionary*). Those having idiosyncratic meanings will be listed, of course, and perhaps those displaying allomorphy as well; but those that are entirely regular or compositional in form and meaning would not be included, as this would only encumber the speaker's memory alongside the truly idiosyncratic forms of the language.

Chapter 2

1. The claim made here that these sorts of compounds (and those under (2.3a,b,d)) are missing from English will be defended below.

2. Note the absence from (2.1d) of the exocentric compounds *pickpocket, sawbones,* etc., which are structurally identical to the others in that list. These will be discussed in section 2.2.3.

3. But note the existence of *chain-smoker*.

4. To avoid the conclusion that (2.5) is a part of the grammar of English, it would have to be possible to explain the gaps in the paradigm in terms of some other principles—for example, principles that might link the existence of certain compound types to the particularities of the syntactic structure of the language. At present, I do not know what such principles might be, but the idea is obviously worth considering.

5. Note that in Allen's (1978, 101) IS A Condition, the right-headedness of compounds is given expression.

6. This formulation of Percolation will be revised in section 3.2.3.

7. Note that strict subcategorization features are not assumed to form part of the category name, and hence do not percolate. Good evidence exists that in word structure the strict subcategorization features of a head are not those of the mother node; see section 2.3.2.

8. There are of course cases that do not involve the subset relation. For example, we find "coordinative" compounds such as *toy gun,* where neither constituent modifies the other. I am grateful to Roger Higgins for reminding me of this fact.

9. Roeper and Siegel (1978) use the term *verbal compound* in a slightly different sense. The difference will become clear as we proceed.

10. See Botha (1980) for a study of verbal compounds in Afrikaans, which takes issue with Roeper and Siegel's approach.

11. See Levi (1978), who also argues for certain subgeneralizations in the semantics of compounds.

12. Roger Higgins has pointed out to me that a certain class of compounds with particles poses a problem for the sort of rewriting rule treatment I am proposing. The class involves deverbal agent nouns followed by a particle, such as *runner up (of little bills), hanger on, screwer down,* etc. Such locutions are well attested in English (see Lindelöf (1935)). The problem is that these agent nouns will exist only if the corresponding verb–particle construction does, yet there is no way that the verb–particle construction forms a constituent to which the agentive suffix attaches. Thus, some other sort of relation must be established between lexical items having the structures (i) and (ii), one that combines them in still another way.

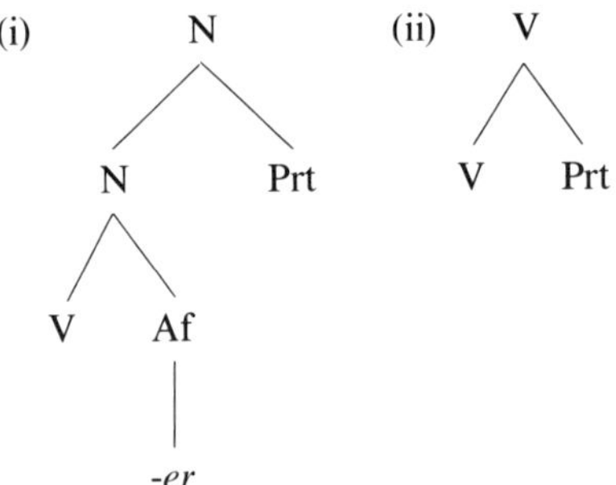

13. There are examples like *consumer spending* and *state borrowing,* pointed out to me by T. Roeper, which may appear to be problematic for the generalization that subject arguments do not appear in verbal compounds, for here the left-hand Ns would seem to be interpreted as the (Agent) subjects of the head. However, it is not entirely clear that these locutions *are* compounds, and an analysis in terms of phrasal collocations is not out of the question. Note the possibility of conjoining the noun *state* with the adjective *federal: State and federal borrowing is on the rise. Federal,* too, has an agentive force to it, but this does not require the conclusion that the word is a noun; we are inclined to assign it the status of a prenominal adjectival modifier in phrase structure, and would therefore do the same for *state* in this expression. I will assume that this is the analysis for the apparent counterexamples cited above.

14. I am grateful to Irene Heim for pointing this out to me.

15. A class of examples pointed out to me by T. Roeper, including *cigarette-smoking by children* and *revenue-sharing by local communities,* is seemingly problematic for the FOPC as stated. The Agent argument, which is a second argument of the deverbal forms here, may be realized within the NP even though the deverbal noun is embedded within a compound. I am not certain what the consequences are of these examples. Perhaps the FOPC is too general and should be stated with respect to arguments of particular types. Or perhaps it is entirely misguided and should be replaced by a different sort of principle altogether. Unfortunately, I have not had the opportunity to investigate this issue, and I will not pursue it here.

16. I assume that the pluralized prepositions to be found in examples like *the ups and downs, the ins and outs,* pointed out to me by Roger Higgins, are instances of deprepositional nouns.

17. The *u* of *u plur* means 'unmarked for _____' and is taken to be nondistinct from "+" or "−".

18. In this regard, I should add a remark on Greek compounds such as [[erythro][cyte]], [[tele][scope]]. Following SPE, I will assume that this sort of compounding takes place at a level different from, and "lower" than, Word. In SPE, the internal constituents of such compounds are labeled *Stem*. For reasons to be explained in section 3.3, I will use the term *Root* to designate this category type and give *erythrocyte,* for example, the structure (i):

(i)

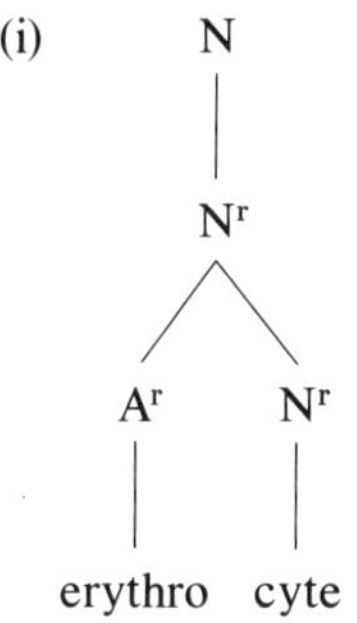

Chapter 3

1. Recall that a noun is a category of level Word with nominal features.

2. The requirement that $n \neq$ Af claims in essence that there are no complex affixes, which seems to be true for English. Future research will reveal whether this is appropriate as a general claim.

3. See Liberman and Prince (1977), Kiparsky (1979), Hayes (1980, chapter 5), and Selkirk (forthcoming, chapter 7) for more recent demonstrations of this point.

4. Note that a purely "schematic" $\overline{X}$ approach also shares this deficiency.

5. It is not the case that all inflectional features play a role in the syntax. Certainly conjugational or declensional class features do not.

6. The evidence also points to the inadequacy of the rather different theory of inflection, proposed by Anderson (1977), wherein individual affixes have no categorial status, but are merely sequences of segments introduced by individual "realization" rules.

7. See Williams (1981a) for some discussion.

8. Rather than providing an exhaustive or detailed description of English derivational morphology in this section, I will simply sketch the gross outlines, which are sufficient, I think, to the theoretical questions at hand. For definitive descriptive treatments of English derivational morphology, see Marchand (1969) and Jespersen (1954).

9. So, for example, the fact that the *m* of *rhythm* is syllabic before the neutral *-y* (*rhythmy*) but not before the nonneutral *-ic* (*rhythmic*) is to be attributed to the fact that the *m* "syllabifies with" *-ic,* but not with *-y*. Not all of the differences in the segmental phonology of words with neutral as opposed to nonneutral affixes can be explained in terms of syllabification, of course. The lack of Velar Softening ($k \rightarrow s$) before the neutral *i*-initial suffixes probably should not be explained in terms of syllabification, but should rather be seen as one of those "marked" or peripheral phonological processes which make appeal to information about morphological structure rather than simply to information about prosodic structure.

10. On the lack of boundaries in phonology, see, for example, Selkirk (1980a, 1980b, forthcoming) and Rotenberg (1978).

11. I should point out that in speaking of a cyclic determination of prosodic structure, I am speaking of the mapping between syntax and phonology, which is the defining or "building" of phonological representation on the basis of syntactic representation. That this mapping is cyclic does not necessarily imply that the application of phonological rules (rules mapping one phonological representation into another) is cyclic. I believe that question is very much unresolved.

12. On categorial grammars, see Ajdukiewicz (1935), Bar-Hillel (1953), and Lambek (1961).

13. Allen (1978) treats *non-* as the first constituent of a compound. She is forced to this unlikely position because in her theory it is the only one consistent with the ability of *non-* to appear outside of compounds.

14. The few instances apparently composed of *un-* plus Noun, e.g., *uninvolvement, unfulfillment, unacceptance, unemployment,* are probably back-formations of some sort; compare *uninvolved, unfulfilled, unaccepted, unemployed.* See Allen (1978, 34) for discussion.

15. The reason that *reroute* is a word (rather than a root) is that it is formed from a denominal verb, $_V[_N[route]_N]_V$; I claim "zero-formation" to be a relation between categories of level Word, not Root.

16. The reason that *-ize* is assumed to be Class II in this instance is that there is no stress on *-dard*. When *-ize* is nonneutral, it is to be expected that a stress will fall on a preceding closed syllable, as in *amortize*. See Hayes (1980, chapter 5).

17. There is another sort of "mixed" theory which (similar to *Syntactic Structures*) would allow for a variety of affix categories—for example, Af^N for noun-taking suffixes, Af^V for verb-taking suffixes, etc.—and would thus not require the strict subcategorization of affixes. See Chomsky (1965) for arguments against this kind of theory.

18. I will simply outline a final type of argument in favor of the categorial status of affixes. It would also involve demonstrating that diacritic features must be assigned to affixes themselves, and would be based on the operation of allomorphy rules which are governed by diacritic features, such as those playing a role in inflection. Further, the argument would involve showing that, in order to properly characterize the context in which some rule of allomorphy applies, it is not enough that the mother node dominating an affix or sequence of affixes be specified in terms of some feature or features; rather, the specification must be "localized" on the affix itself (or affixes themselves). Readers are invited to draw on their experience and ascertain whether such cases do exist. If so, then this type of argument may be added to the others I have given in support of the categorial status of affixes.

19. Though, in fact, not all bound morphemes are affixes, e.g., *moll-* of *mollify*, *cran-* of *cranberry*, etc.

References

Adams, V. (1973). *An Introduction to Modern English Word Formation*, Longman, London.

Ajdukiewicz, K. (1935). "Die syntaktische Konnexität," *Studia Philosophica*, 1, 1–27. (Appears in English translation in S. McCall, ed. (1967). *Polish Logic*, Oxford University Press, Oxford.)

Allen, M. (1978). *Morphological Investigations*, Doctoral dissertation, University of Connecticut, Storrs, Connecticut.

Anderson, S. (1977). "On the Formal Description of Inflection," in W. A. Beach, S. E. Fox, and S. Philosoph, eds., *Papers from the Thirteenth Regional Meeting of the Chicago Linguistic Society*, University of Chicago, Chicago, Illinois.

Aronoff, M. (1974). "*-able*," in J. Hankamer and E. Kaisse, eds., *Papers from the Fifth Annual Meeting of the North Eastern Linguistic Society*, Harvard University, Cambridge, Massachusetts.

Aronoff, M. (1976). *Word Formation in Generative Grammar*, Linguistic Inquiry Monograph 1, MIT Press, Cambridge, Massachusetts.

Bar-Hillel, Y. (1953). "A Quasi-Arithmetical Notation of Syntactic Description," *Language* 29, 47–58.

Bloomfield, L. (1933). *Language*, Holt, Rinehart and Winston, New York.

Botha, R. P. (1980). "Word-based Morphology and Synthetic Compounding," *Stellenbosch Papers in Linguistics* 5.

Bresnan, J. W. (1976). "On the Form and Functioning of Transformations," *Linguistic Inquiry* 7, 3–40.

Bresnan, J. W. (1979). "Polyadicity: Part I of a Theory of Lexical Rules and Representations," in T. Hoekstra, H. van der Hulst, and M. Moortgat, eds., *Lexical Grammar*, special issue of *GLOT—Leids Taalkundig Bulletin*.

Bresnan, J. W. (1982a). "The Passive in Lexical Theory," in J. W. Bresnan, ed. (1982b).

Bresnan, J. W., ed. (1982b). *The Mental Representation of Grammatical Relations,* MIT Press, Cambridge, Massachusetts.

Chomsky, N. (1957). *Syntactic Structures,* Mouton, The Hague.

Chomsky, N. (1965). *Aspects of the Theory of Syntax,* MIT Press, Cambridge, Massachusetts.

Chomsky, N. (1970). "Remarks on Nominalization," in R. A. Jacobs and P. S. Rosenbaum, eds., *Readings in English Transformational Grammar,* Ginn, Waltham, Massachusetts. Reprinted in N. Chomsky, ed. (1972b).

Chomsky, N. (1972a). "Some Empirical Issues in the Theory of Transformational Grammar," in S. Peters, ed., *The Goals of Linguistic Theory,* Prentice-Hall, Englewood Cliffs, New Jersey. Reprinted in N. Chomsky, ed. (1972b).

Chomsky, N. (1972b). *Studies on Semantics in Generative Grammar,* Mouton, The Hague.

Chomsky, N., and M. Halle (1968). *The Sound Pattern of English,* Harper and Row, New York.

Clark, M. (1978). *A Dynamic Treatment of Tone with Special Attention to the Tonal System of Igbo,* Doctoral dissertation, University of Massachusetts. Distributed by the Indiana University Linguistics Club, Bloomington, Indiana.

Dell, F. (1970). *Les règles phonologiques tardives et la morphologie dérivationnelle du français,* Doctoral dissertation, MIT, Cambridge, Massachusetts.

Dell, F. (1979). "La morphologie dérivationnelle du français et l'organisation de la composante lexicale en grammaire générative," *Revue Romane* XIV, 185–216.

Dell, F., and E. O. Selkirk (1978). "On a Morphologically Governed Vowel Alternation in French," in S. J. Keyser, ed., *Recent Transformational Studies in European Linguistics,* Linguistic Inquiry Monograph 3, MIT Press, Cambridge, Massachusetts.

Downing, P. (1977). "On the Creation and Use of English Compound Nouns," *Language* 53, 810–842.

Dowty, D. (1979). *Word Meaning and Montague Grammar,* Reidel, Dordrecht.

Emonds, J. (1976). *A Transformational Approach to English Syntax,* Academic Press, New York.

Green, M. M., and G. E. Igwe (1963). *A Descriptive Grammar of Igbo,* Oxford University Press, Oxford.

Grévisse, M. (1969). *Le bon usage,* 9e édition, Hatier, Paris.

Grimshaw, J. (1982). "On the Lexical Representation of Romance Reflexive Clitics," in J. W. Bresnan, ed. (1982b).

Gruber, J. (1965). *Studies in Lexical Relations,* Doctoral dissertation, MIT, Cambridge, Massachusetts. Distributed by the Indiana University Linguistics Club, Bloomington, Indiana.

Halle, M. (1973). "Prolegomena to a Theory of Word Formation," *Linguistic Inquiry* 4, 3–16.

Hayes, B. (1980). *A Metrical Theory of Stress Rules,* Doctoral dissertation, MIT, Cambridge, Massachusetts.

Hoekstra, T., H. van der Hulst, and M. Moortgat, eds. (1979). *Lexical Grammar,* special issue of *GLOT—Leids Taalkundig Bulletin.* (Published 1980 by Foris, Dordrecht.)

Hoijer, H. (1946). "Tonkawa," in H. Hoijer et al., *Linguistic Structures of Native America,* Viking Fund Publcations in Anthropology 6, 289–311.

Hornstein, N., and A. Weinberg (1981). "Case Theory and Preposition Stranding," *Linguistic Inquiry* 12, 55–92.

Igwe, G. E., and M. M. Green (1967). *Igbo Language Course: Book 1,* Igbo Language Study, Oxford University Press, Ibadan, Nigeria.

Jackendoff, R. (1972). *Semantic Interpretation in Generative Grammar,* MIT Press, Cambridge, Massachusetts.

Jackendoff, R. (1975). "Morphological and Semantic Regularities in the Lexicon," *Language* 51, 639–671.

Jackendoff, R. (1977). *$\bar{X}$ Syntax: A Study of Phrase Structure,* Linguistic Inquiry Monograph 2, MIT Press, Cambridge, Massachusetts.

Jaeggli, O. (1980). "Spanish Diminutives," in F. H. Nuessel, Jr., ed., *Contemporary Studies in Romance Languages,* Indiana University Linguistics Club, Bloomington, Indiana.

Jespersen, O. (1954). *A Modern English Grammar on Historical Principles,* George Allen & Unwin, London, and Ejnar Munksgaard, Copenhagen.

Kaplan, R., and J. W. Bresnan (1982). "Lexical-Functional Grammar: A Formal System for Grammatical Representation," in J. W. Bresnan, ed. (1982b).

Kayne, R. S. (1975). *French Syntax,* MIT Press, Cambridge, Massachusetts.

Kenstowicz, M., and C. Kisseberth (1977). *Topics in Phonological Theory,* Academic Press, New York.

Kiparsky, P. (1979). "Metrical Structure Assignment Is Cyclic," *Linguistic Inquiry* 10, 421–442.

Lambek, J. (1961). "On the Calculus of Syntactic Types," in R. Jakobson, ed., *Structure of Language and its Mathematical Aspects,* Proceedings of Symposia in Applied Mathematics XII, American Mathematical Society, Providence, Rhode Island.

Lapointe, S. G. (1978). "A Nontransformational Approach to French Clitics," in *Proceedings of the Ninth Annual Meeting of the North East Linguistic Society,* Queens College Press, New York.

Lapointe, S. (1980a). *A Theory of Grammatical Agreement,* Doctoral dissertation, University of Massachusetts, Amherst.

Lapointe, S. (1980b). "The Representation of Inflectional Morphology within the Lexicon," in V. Burke and J. Pustejovsky, ed., *Proceedings of the Eleventh Annual Meeting of the North East Linguistic Society,* GLSA University of Massachusetts, Amherst.

Lees, R. B. (1960). *The Grammar of English Nominalizations,* Mouton, The Hague.

Levi, J. (1978). *The Syntax and Semantics of Complex Nominals,* Academic Press, New York.

Liberman, M., and A. Prince (1977). "On Stress and Linguistic Rhythm," *Linguistic Inquiry* 8, 249–336.

Lieber, R. (1980). *On the Organization of the Lexicon,* Doctoral dissertation, MIT, Cambridge, Massachusetts.

Lindelöf, U. (1935). "English Agent-nouns with a Suffixed Adverb," *Neuphilologische Mitteilungen* 36, 257–282.

McCarthy, J. (1979). *Formal Problems in Semitic Phonology and Morphology,* Doctoral dissertation, MIT, Cambridge, Massachusetts.

McCarthy, J. (1981). "A Prosodic Theory of Nonconcatenative Morphology," *Linguistic Inquiry* 12, 373–418.

Marchand, H. (1969). *The Categories and Types of Present-Day English Word-Formation,* second edition, C. H. Beck'sche Verlagsbuchhandlung, Munich.

Mohanan, K. P. (1982). *Lexical Phonology,* Doctoral dissertation, MIT, Cambridge, Massachusetts.

Morin, Y.-C. (1978). "Interprétation des pronoms et des réfléchis en français," *Cahiers de Linguistique de l'UQUAM,* Montreal.

Newman, S. S. (1946). "On the Stress System of English," *Word* 2, 171–187.

Newnham, R. (1971). *About Chinese,* Penguin Books, London.

Rivas, A. (1977). *A Theory of Clitics,* Doctoral dissertation, MIT, Cambridge, Massachusetts.

Roeper, T., and M. E. A. Siegel (1978). "A Lexical Transformation for Verbal Compounds," *Linguistic Inquiry* 9, 199–260.

Rotenberg, J. (1978). *The Syntax of Phonology,* Doctoral dissertation, MIT, Cambridge, Massachusetts.

Sapir, E. (1911). "The Problem of Noun Incorporation in American Languages," *American Anthropologist* 13, 250–282.

Selkirk, E. O. (1978). "On Prosodic Structure and its Relation to Syntactic Structure," paper presented at the Sloan Foundation Workshop on the Mental Representation of Phonology, University of Massachusetts, Amherst, November 18–19, 1979. Distributed by the Indiana University Linguistics Club, Bloomington, Indiana.

Selkirk, E. O. (1980a). "The Role of Prosodic Categories in English Word Stress," *Linguistic Inquiry* 11, 563–605.

Selkirk, E. O. (1980b). "Prosodic Domains in Phonology: Sanskrit Revisited," in M. Aronoff and M.-L. Kean, eds., *Juncture,* Anima Libri, Saratoga, California.

Selkirk, E. O. (1981). "English Compounding and the Theory of Word Structure," in T. Hoekstra, H. van der Hulst, and M. Moortgat, eds., *The Scope of Lexical Rules,* special issue of *GLOT—Leids Taalkundig Bulletin.*

Selkirk, E. O. (forthcoming). *Phonology and Syntax: The Relation between Sound and Structure,* MIT Press, Cambridge, Massachusetts.

Siegel, D. (1973). "Nonsources of Unpassives," in J. Kimball, ed., *Syntax and Semantics,* Vol. II, Seminar Press, New York.

Siegel, D. (1974). *Topics in English Morphology,* Doctoral dissertation, MIT, Cambridge, Massachusetts.

Siegel, D. (1977). "The Adjacency Condition and the Theory of Morphology," in M. J. Stein, ed., *Proceedings of the Eighth Annual Meeting of the North East Linguistic Society,* University of Massachusetts, Amherst.

Stillings, J. (1975). "The Formulation of Gapping in English as Evidence for Variable Types in Syntactic Transformations," *Linguistic Analysis* 1, 247–274.

Stowell, T. (1981). *Principles of Lexical and Phrasal Structure,* Doctoral dissertation, MIT, Cambridge, Massachusetts.

Strauss, S. (1979a). "Against Boundary Distinctions in English Morphology," *Linguistic Analysis* 5, 387–419.

Strauss, S. (1979b). *Some Principles of Word Structure in English and German,* Doctoral dissertation, CUNY Graduate Center, New York.

Thompson, L. (1965). *A Vietnamese Grammar,* University of Washington Press, Seattle.

Toman, J. (1978–79). "A Fragment of a Theory of Word Syntax," chapter of unpublished dissertation draft.

Vergnaud, J.-R. (1973). "Formal Properties of Lexical Derivations," *Quarterly Progress Report of the Research Laboratory of Electronics,* MIT, no. 108, 279–287.

Welmers, W. E. (1970). "The Derivation of Igbo Verb Bases," *Studies in African Linguistics* 1, 49–59.

Williams, E. (1980). "Predication," *Linguistic Inquiry* 11, 203–238.

Williams, E. (1981a). "On the Notions 'Lexically Related' and 'Head of a Word'," *Linguistic Inquiry* 12, 245–274.

Williams, E. (1981b). "Argument Structure and Morphology," *Linguistic Review* 1, 81–114.